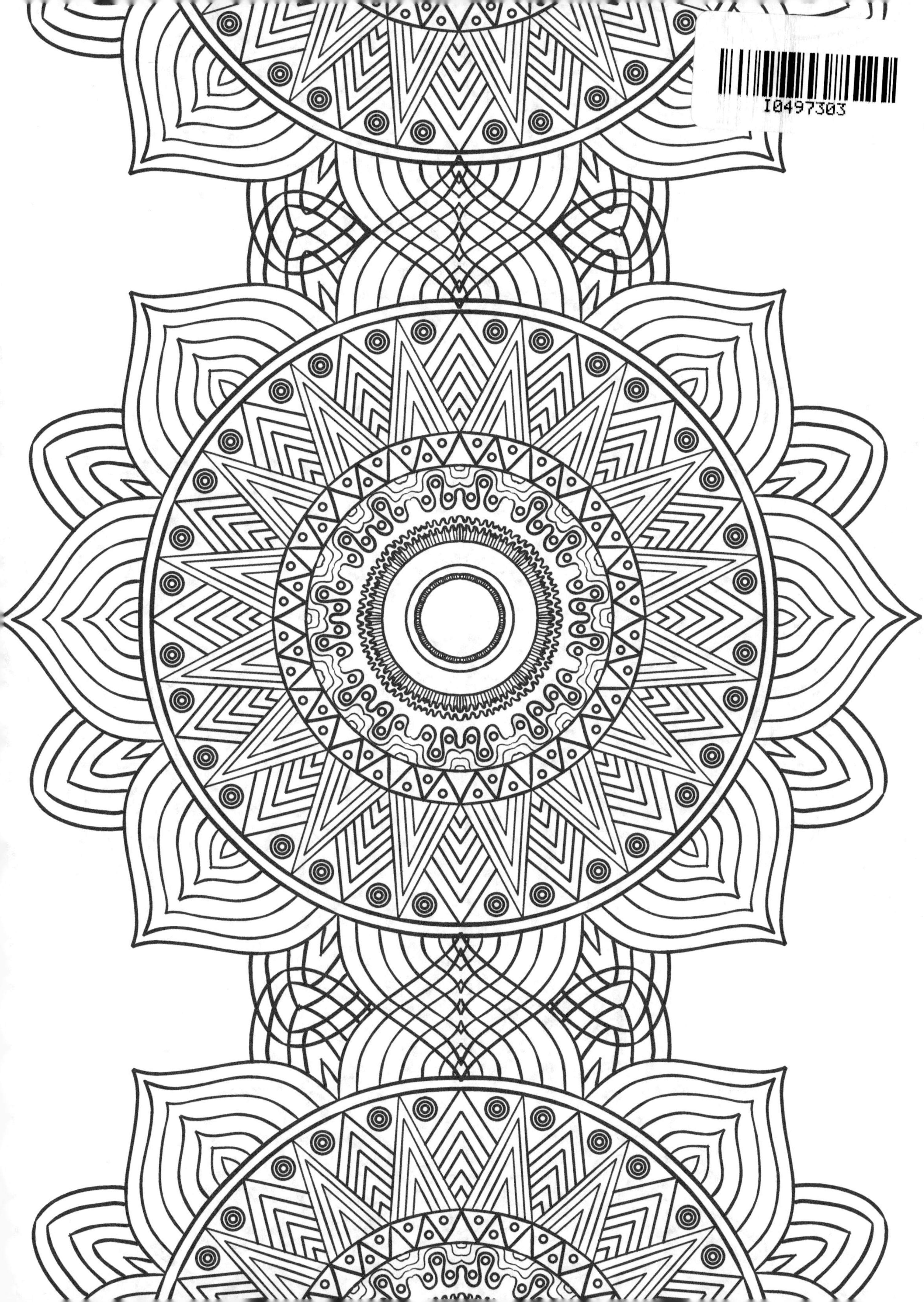

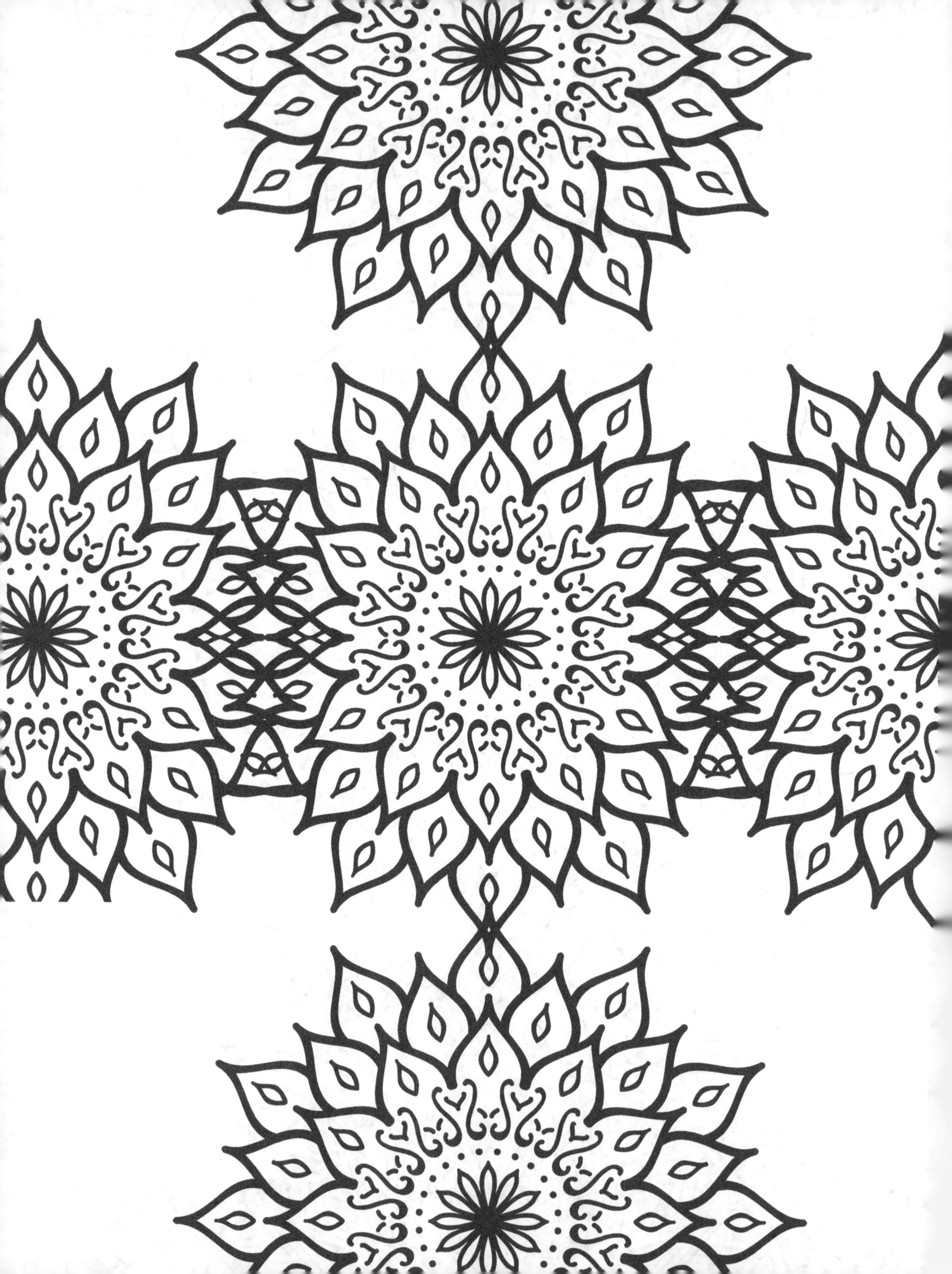

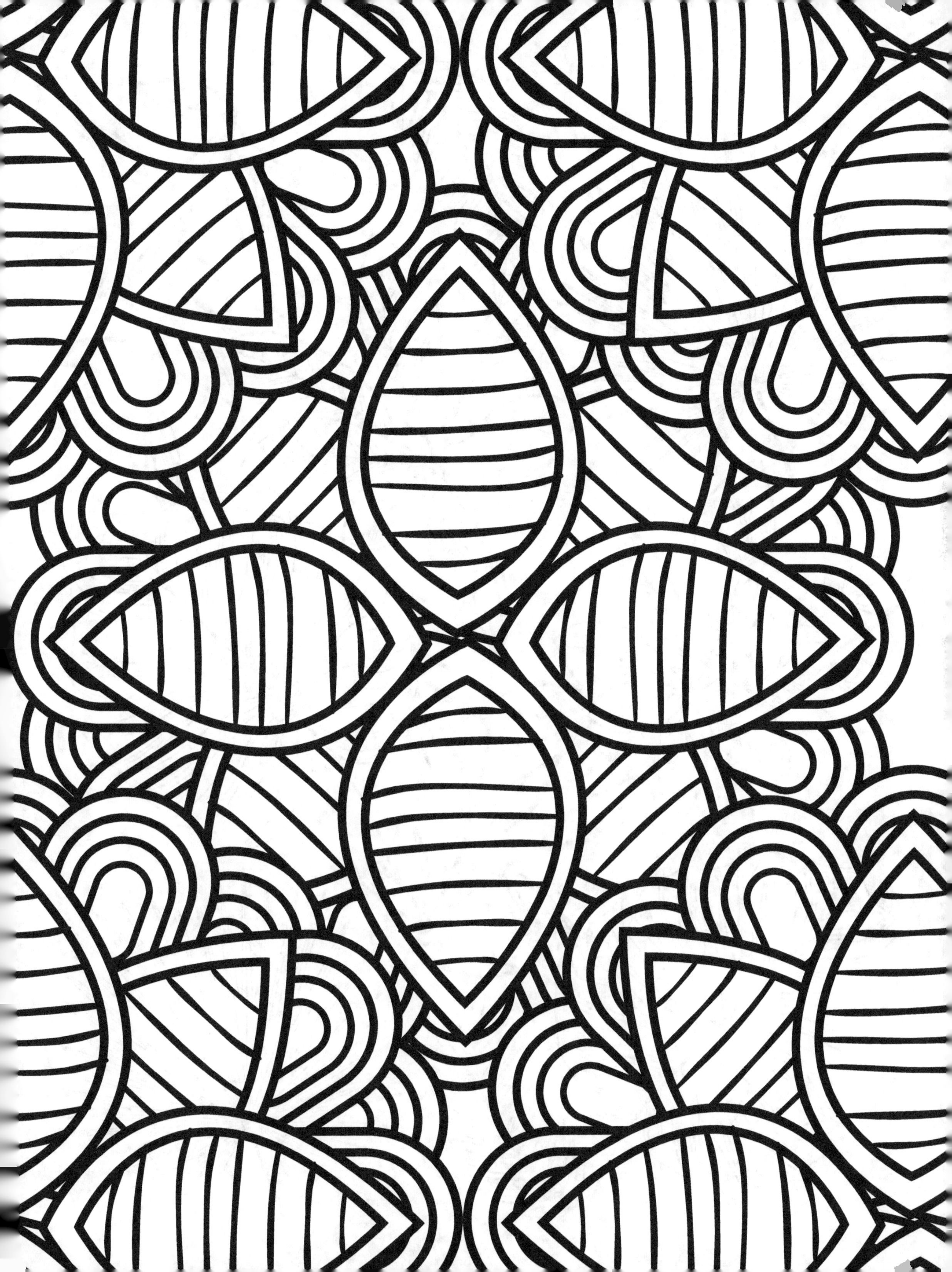

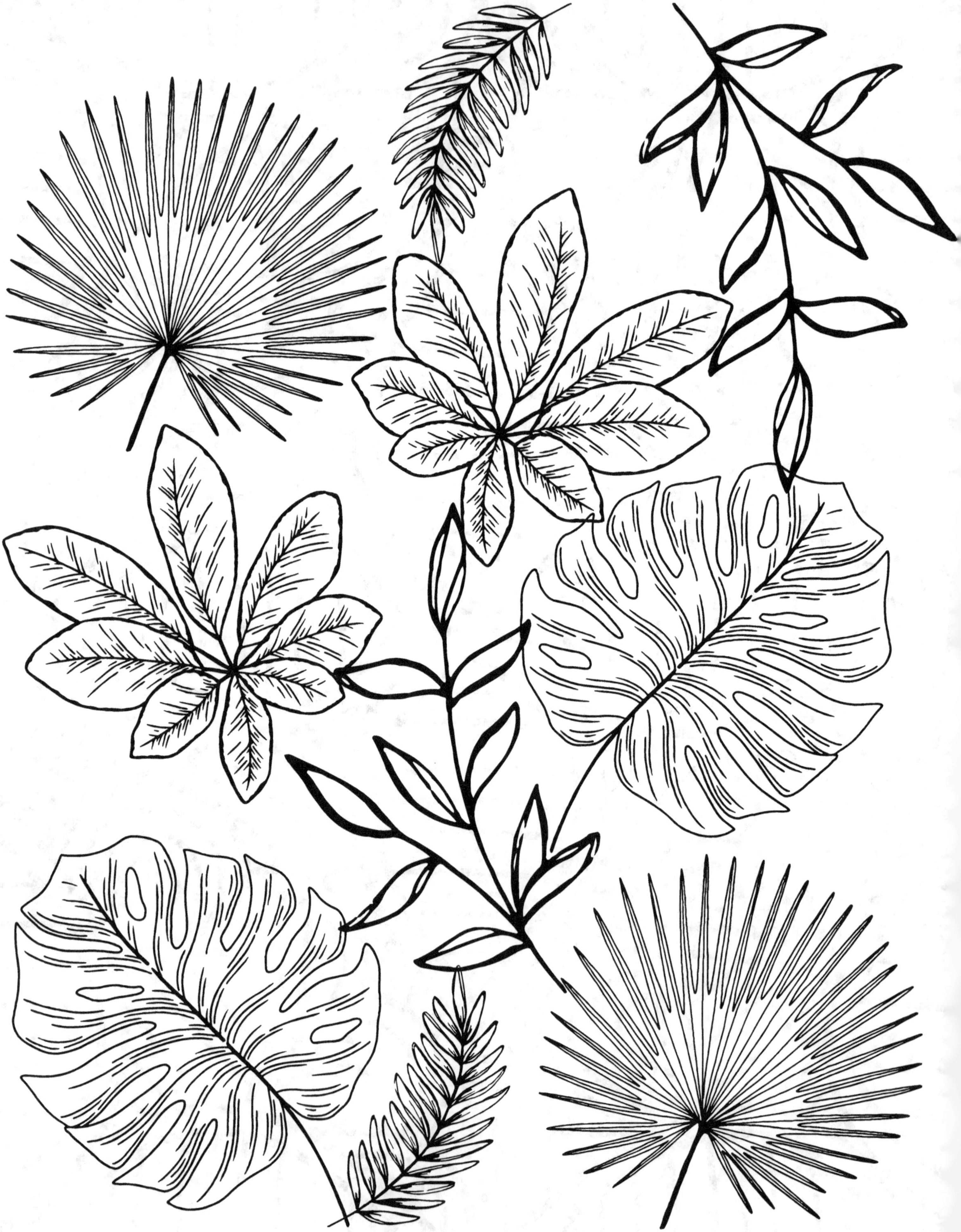

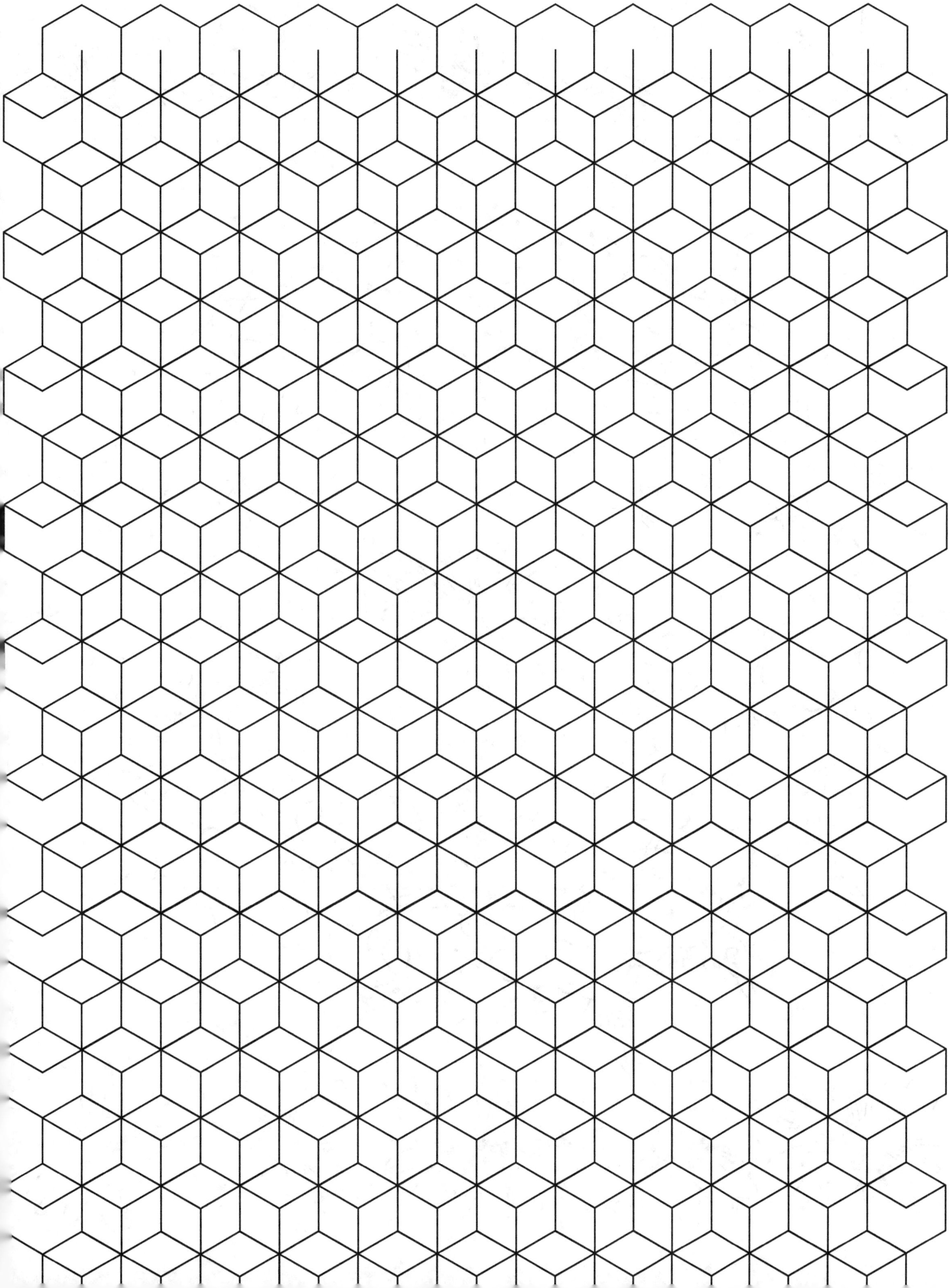

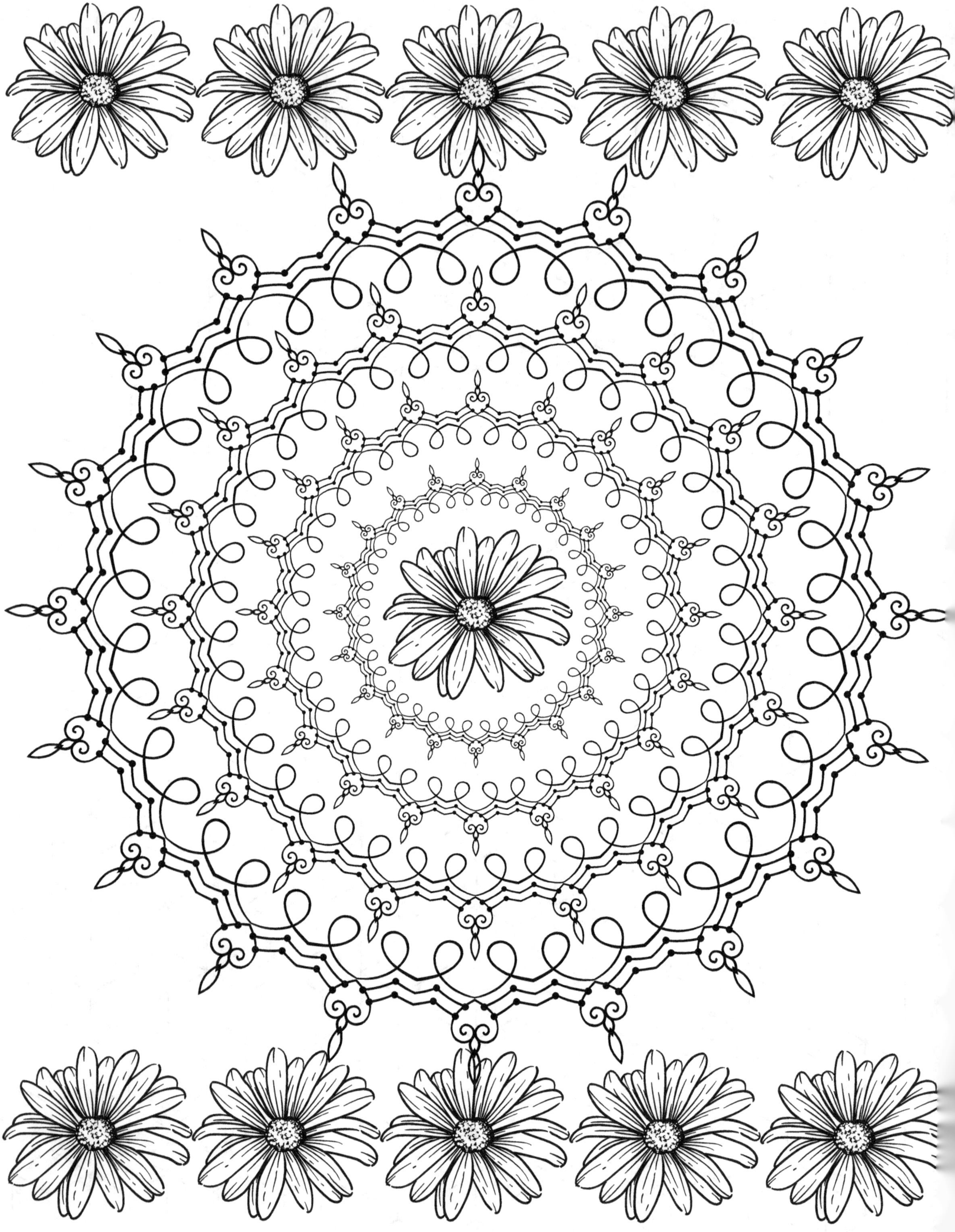

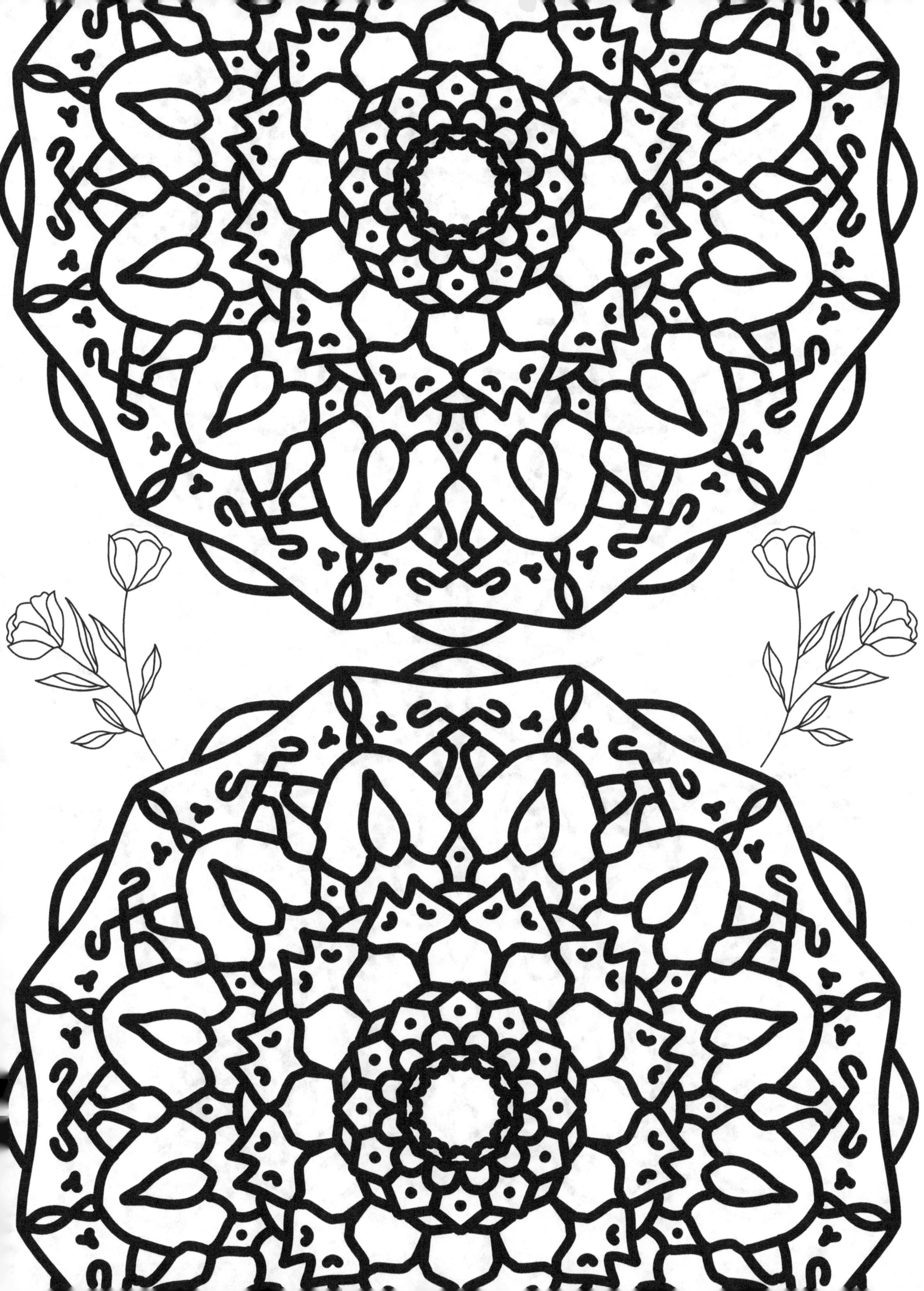

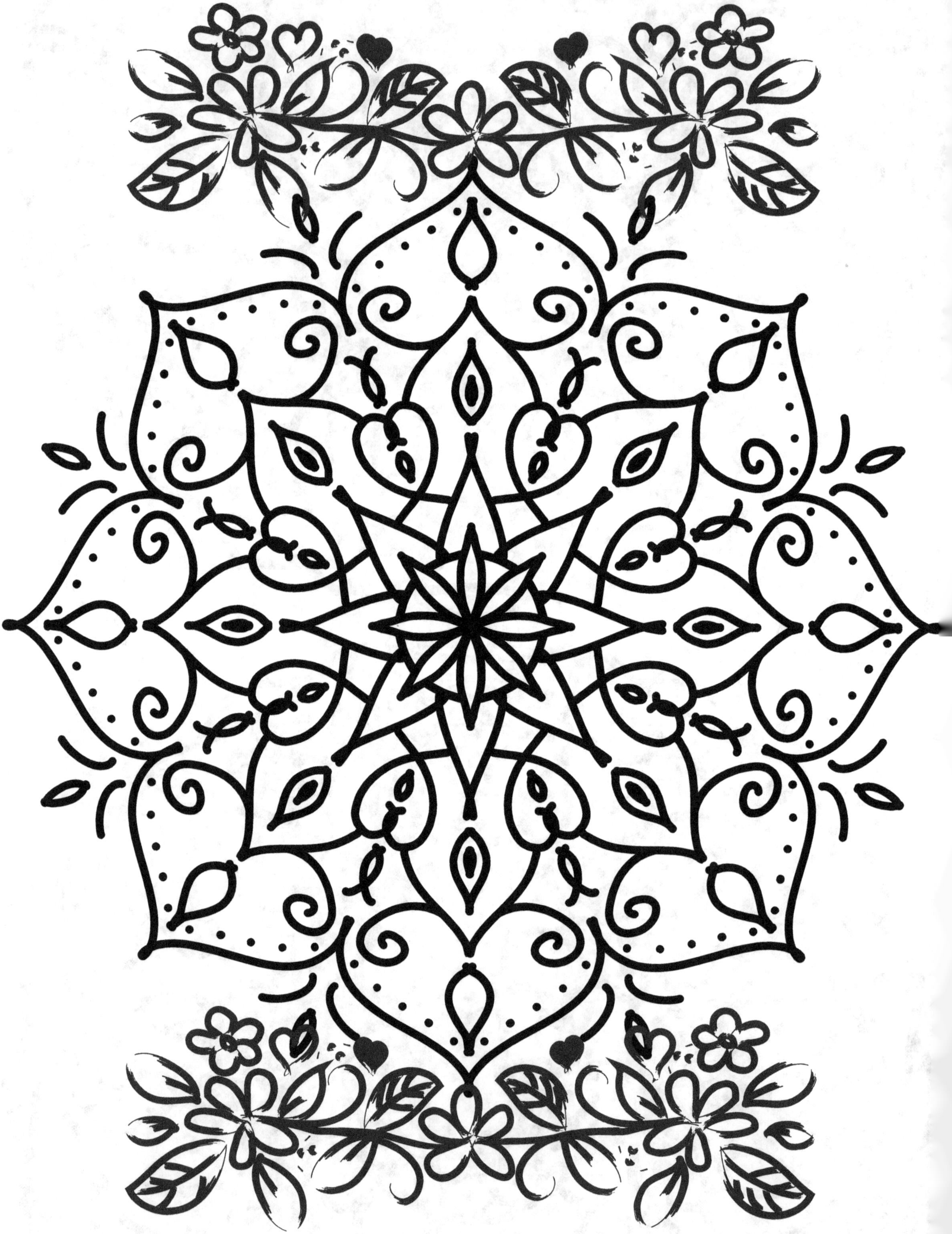

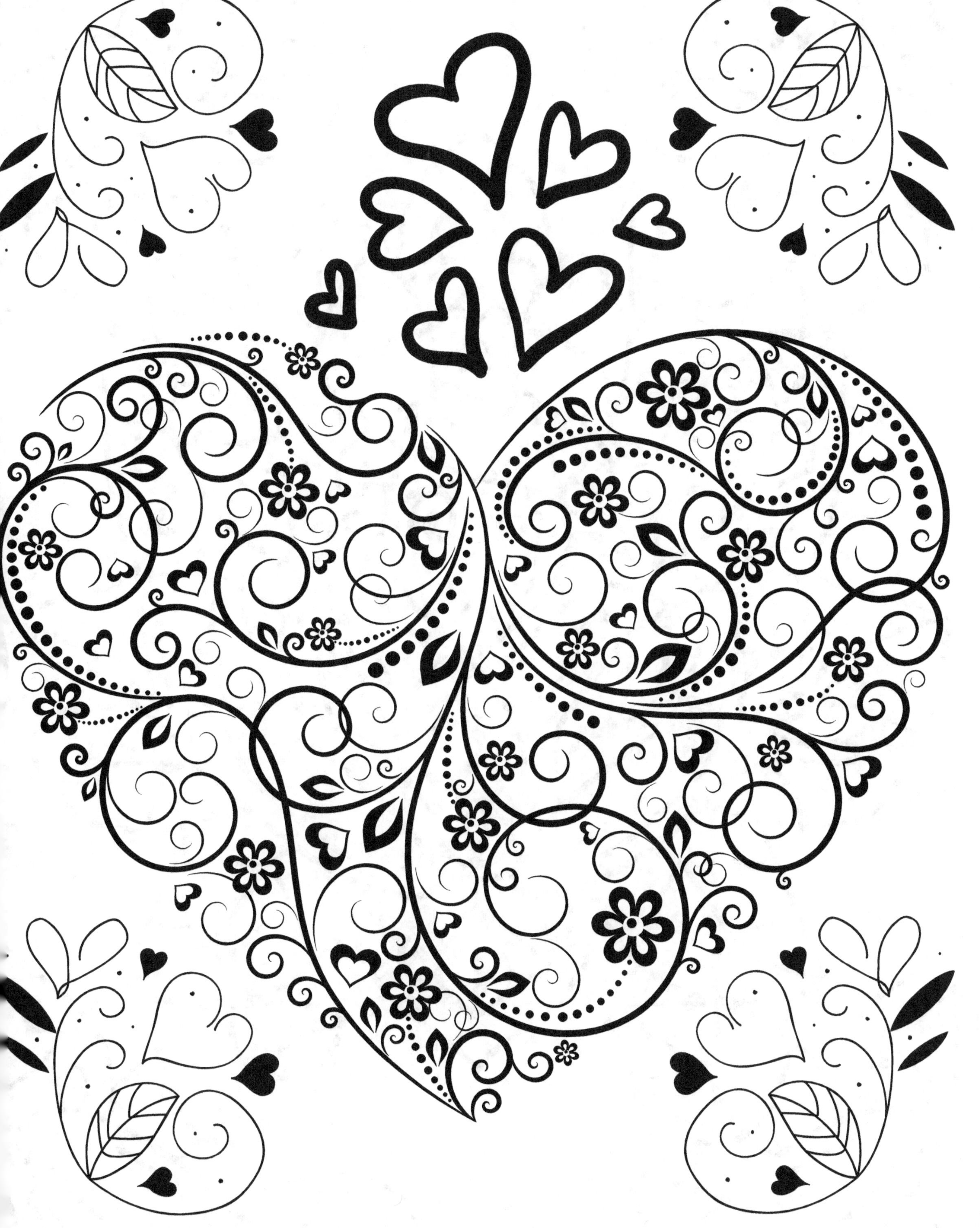

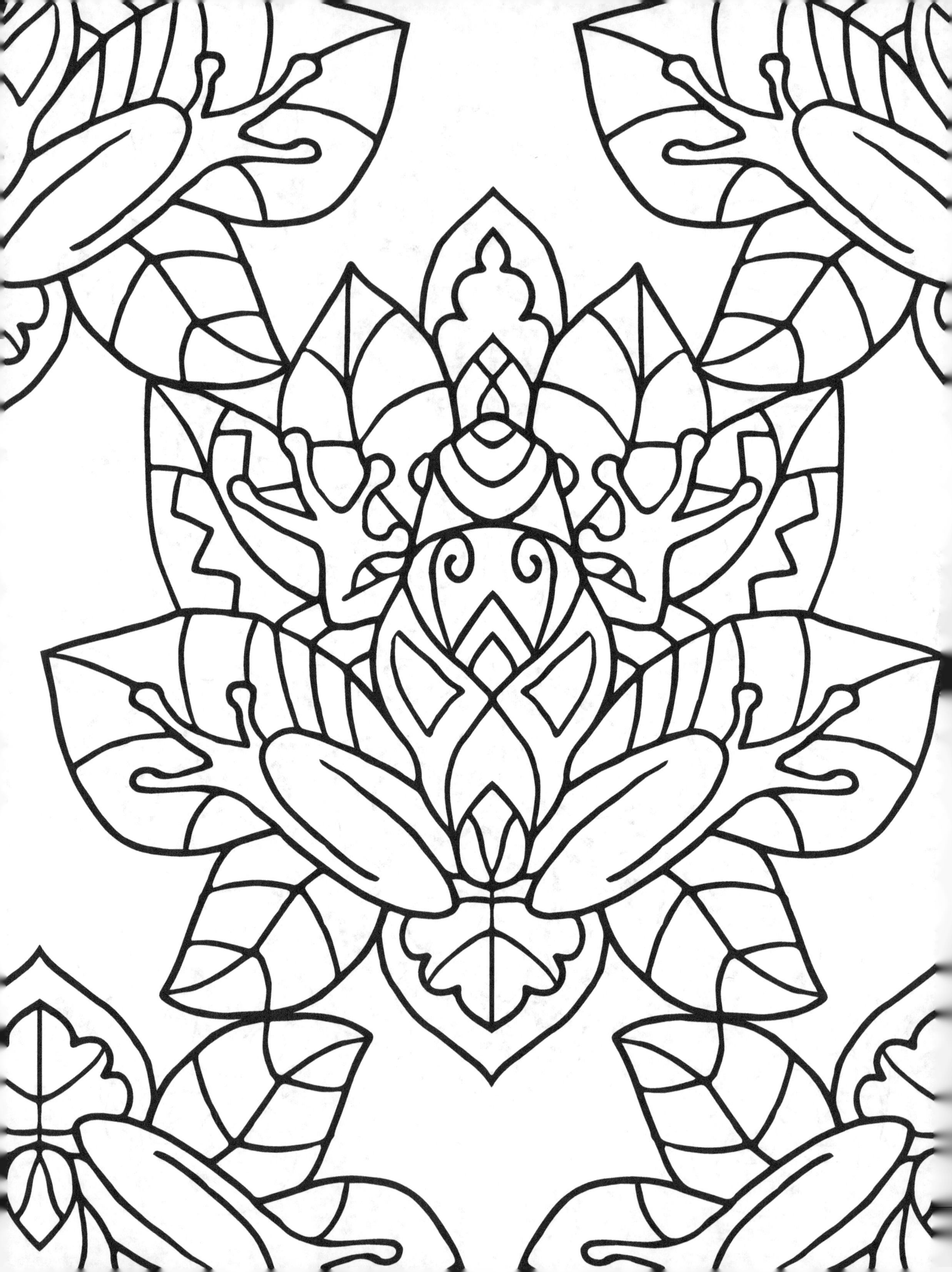

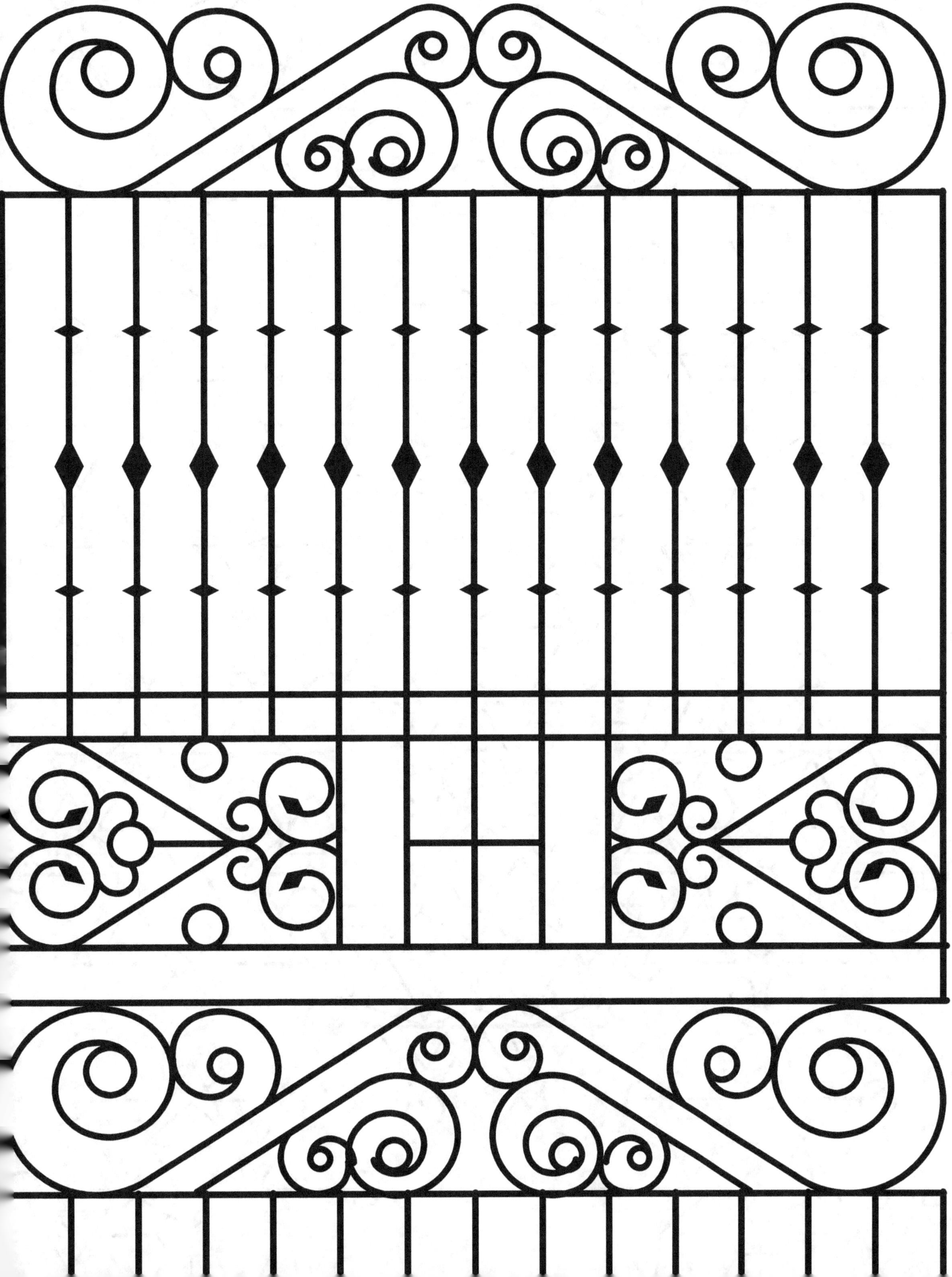

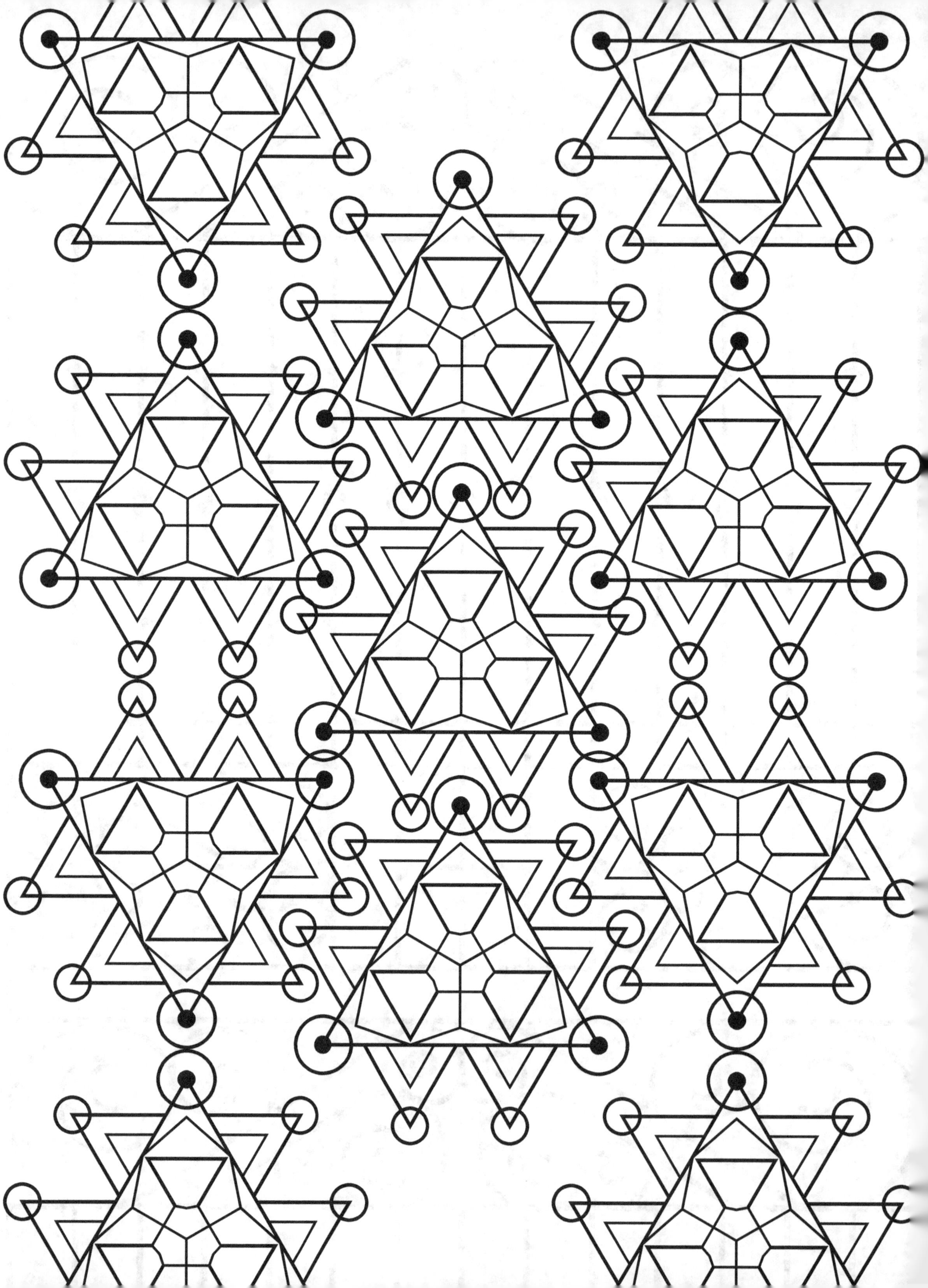

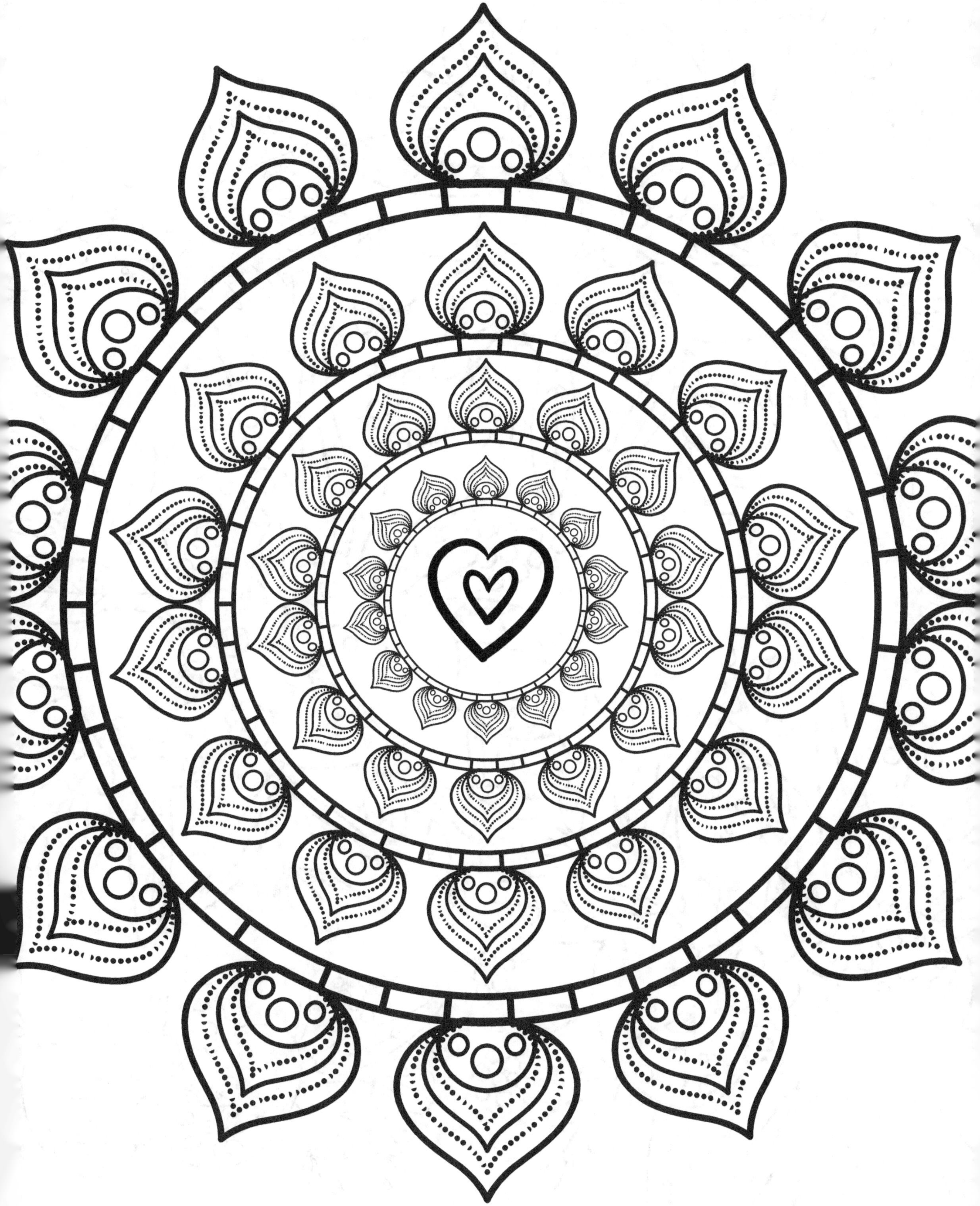

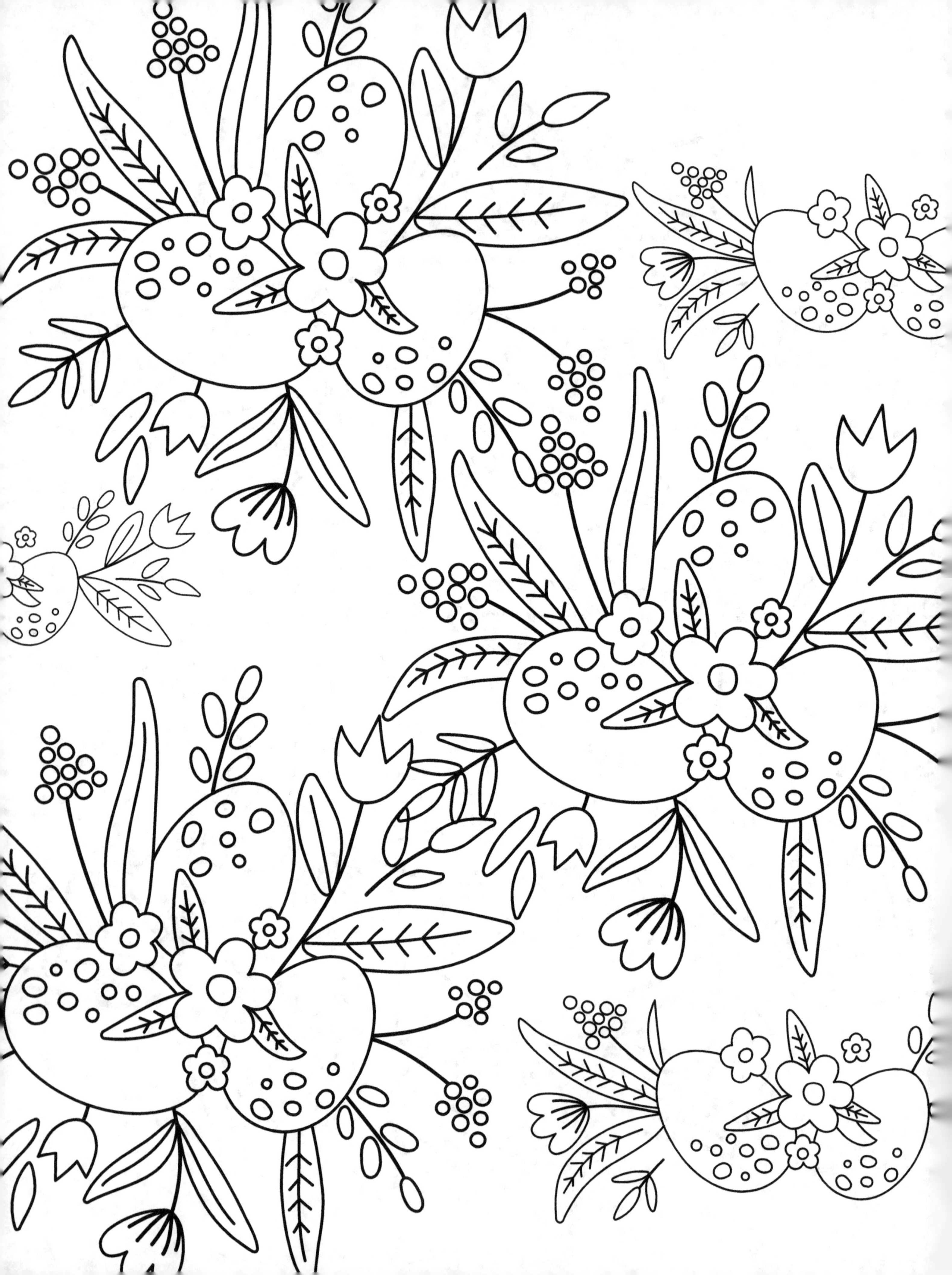

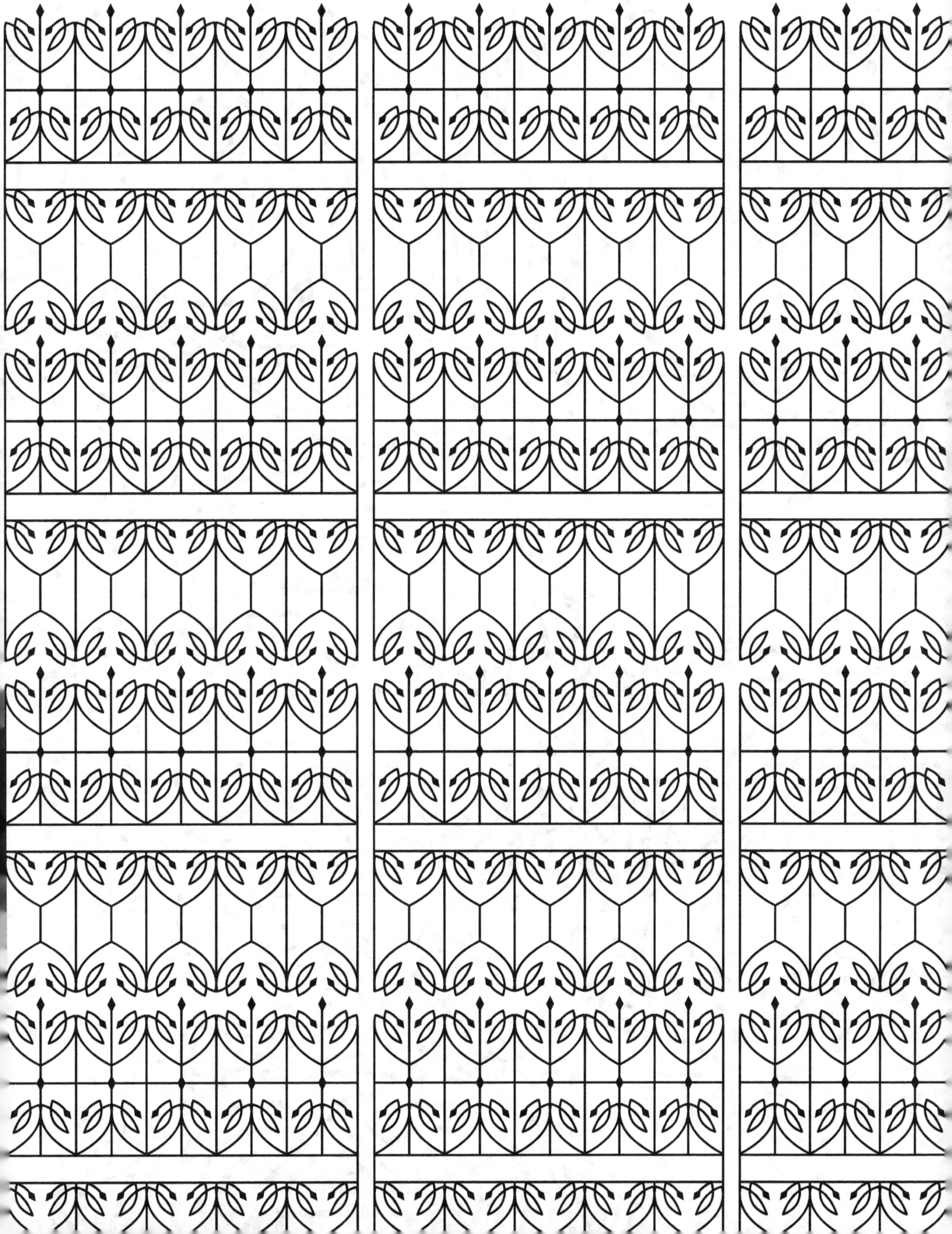

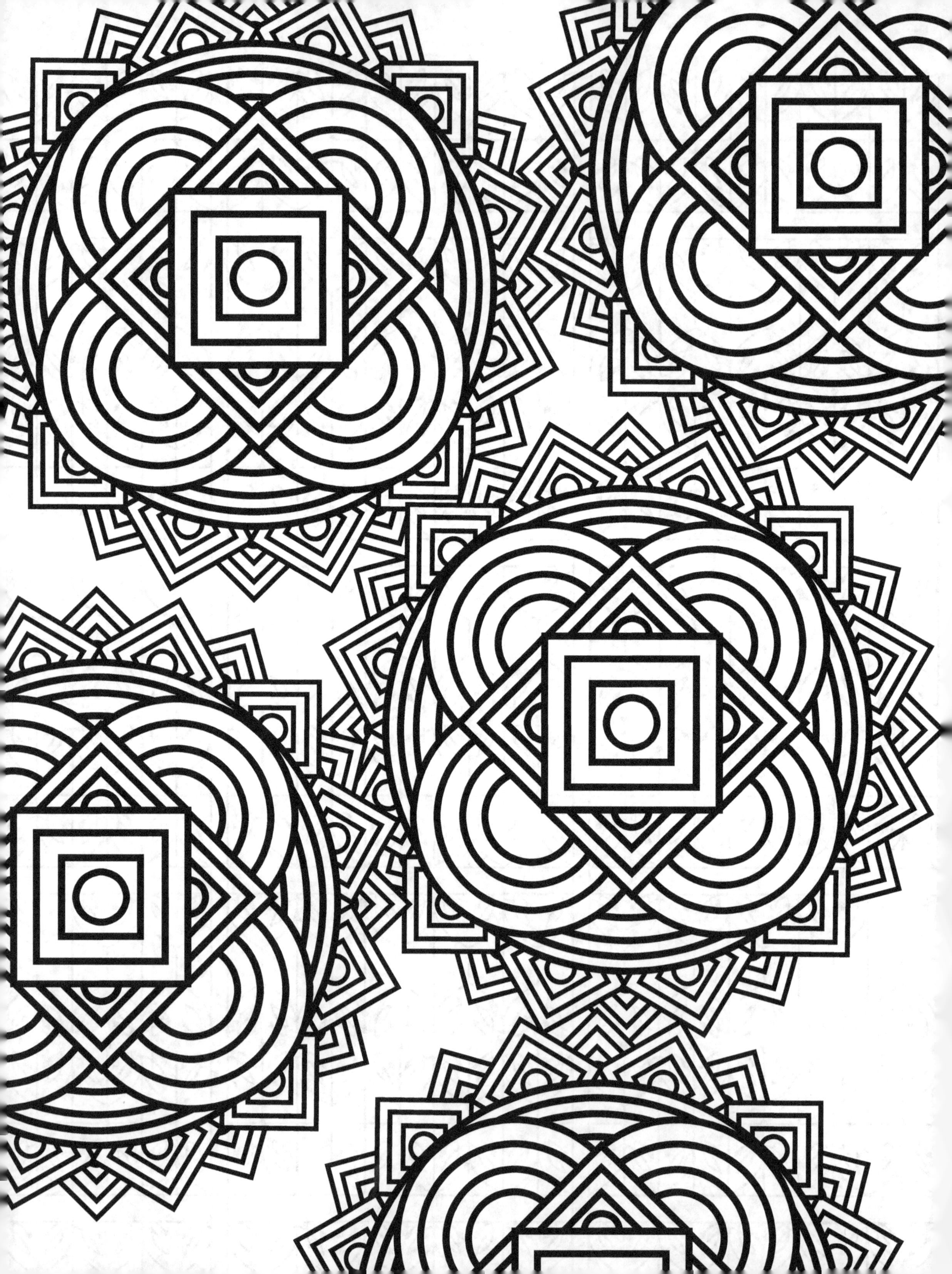

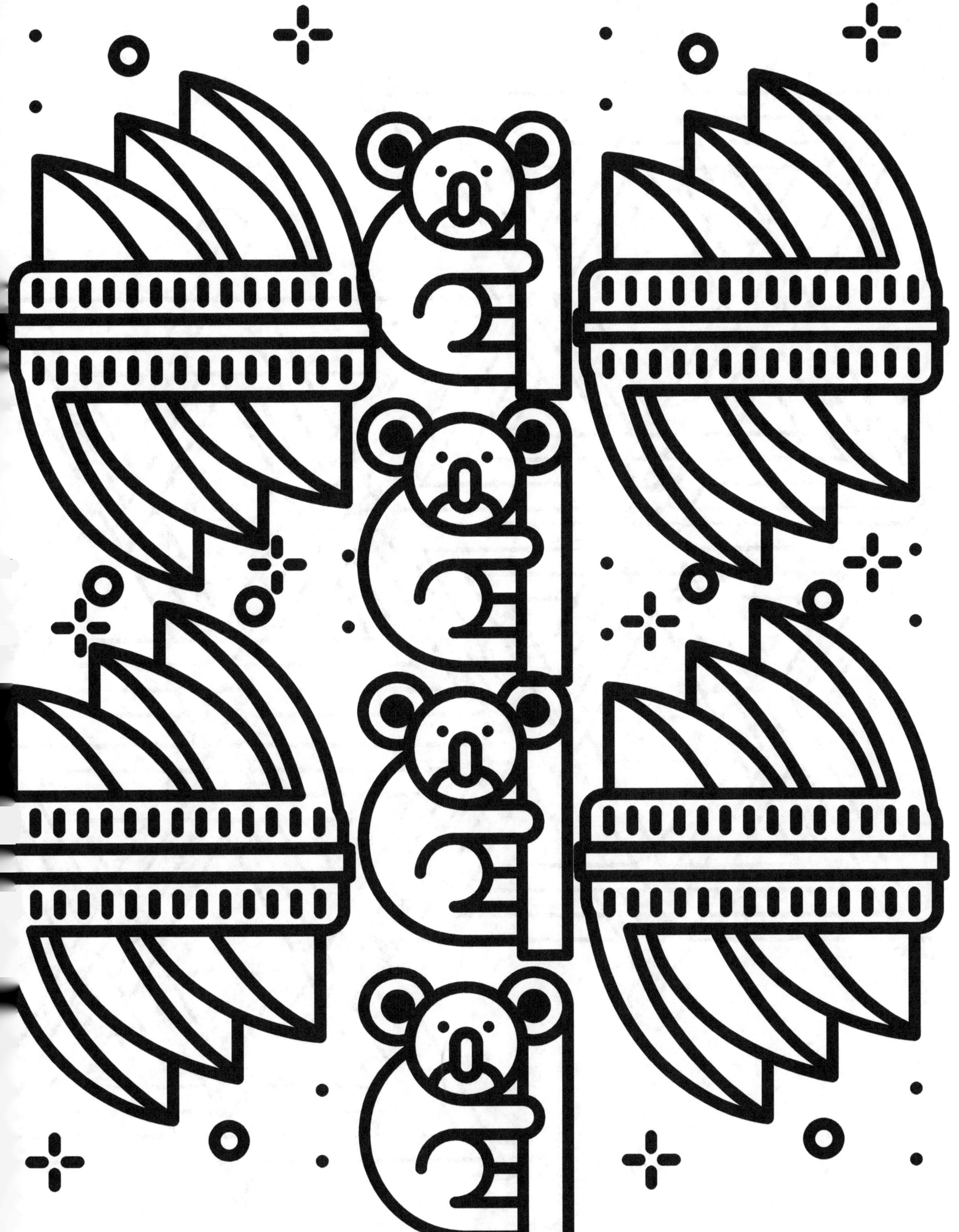

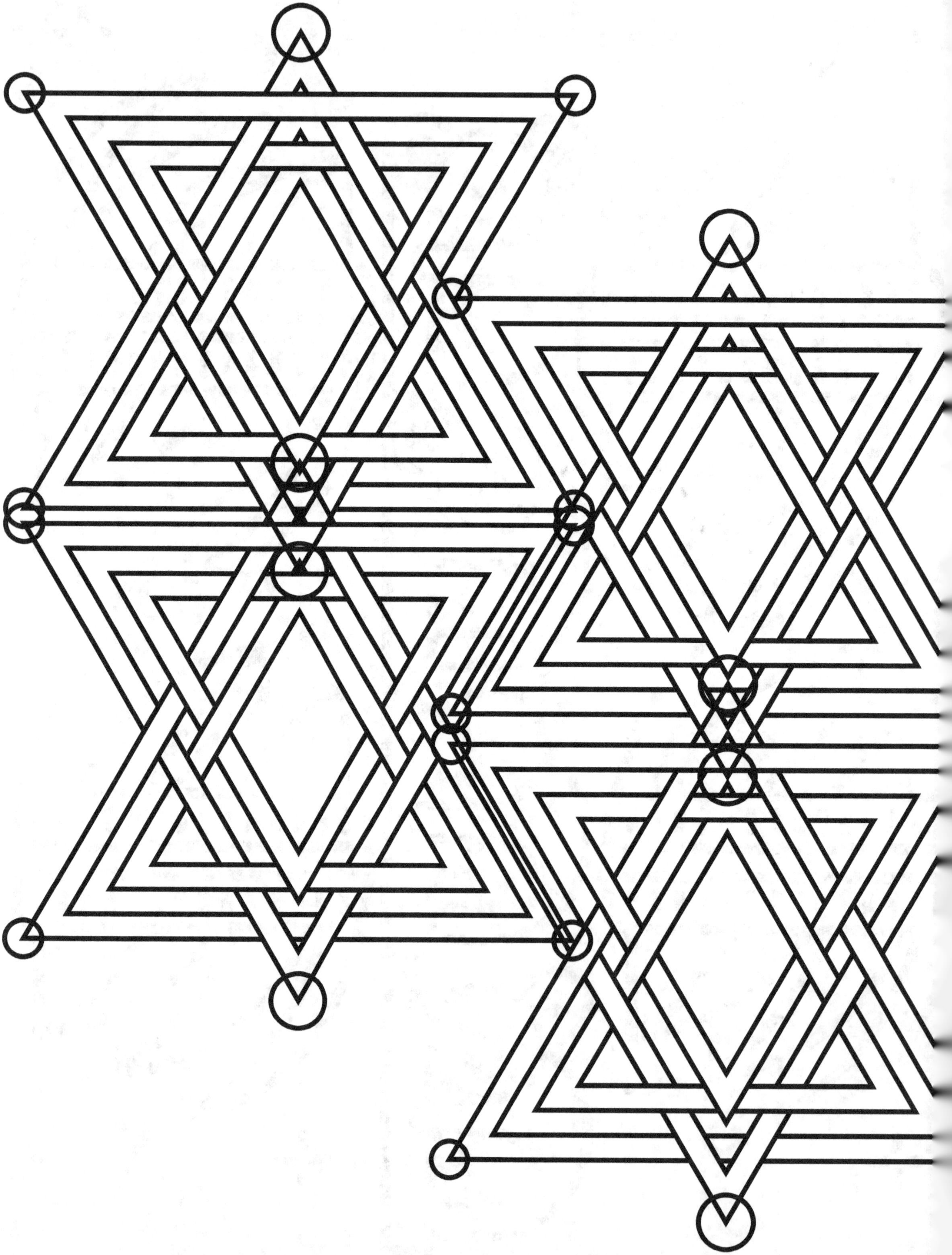

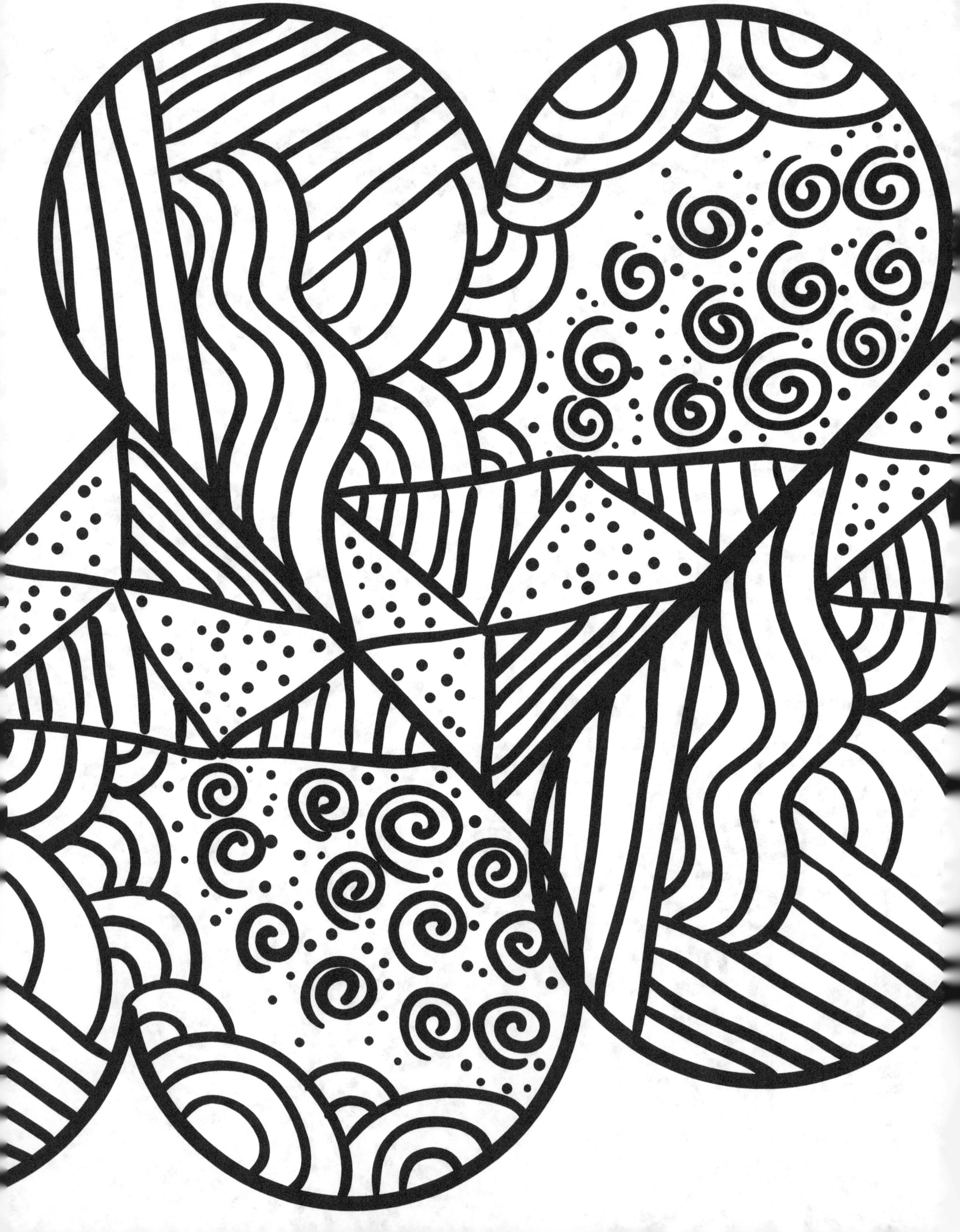

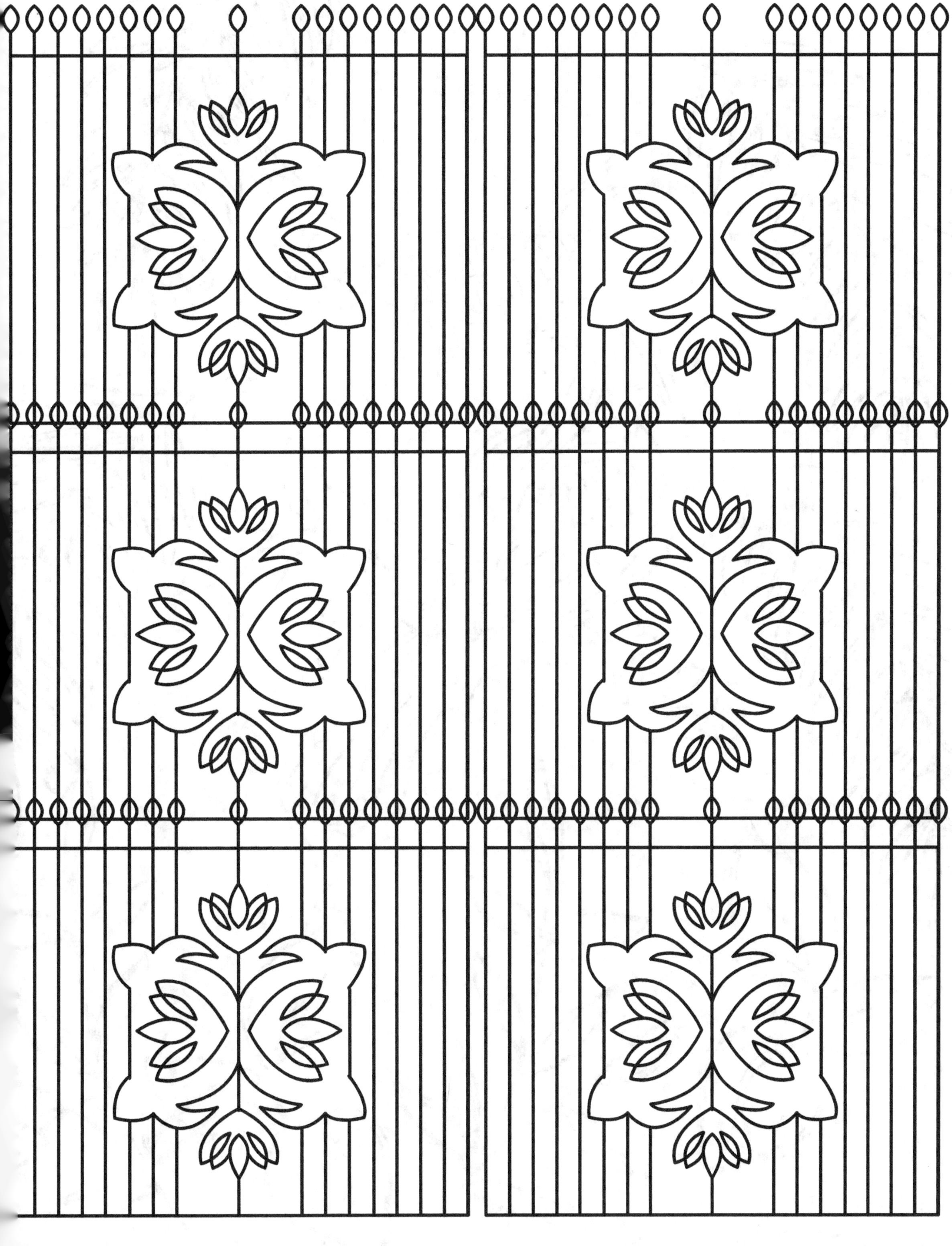

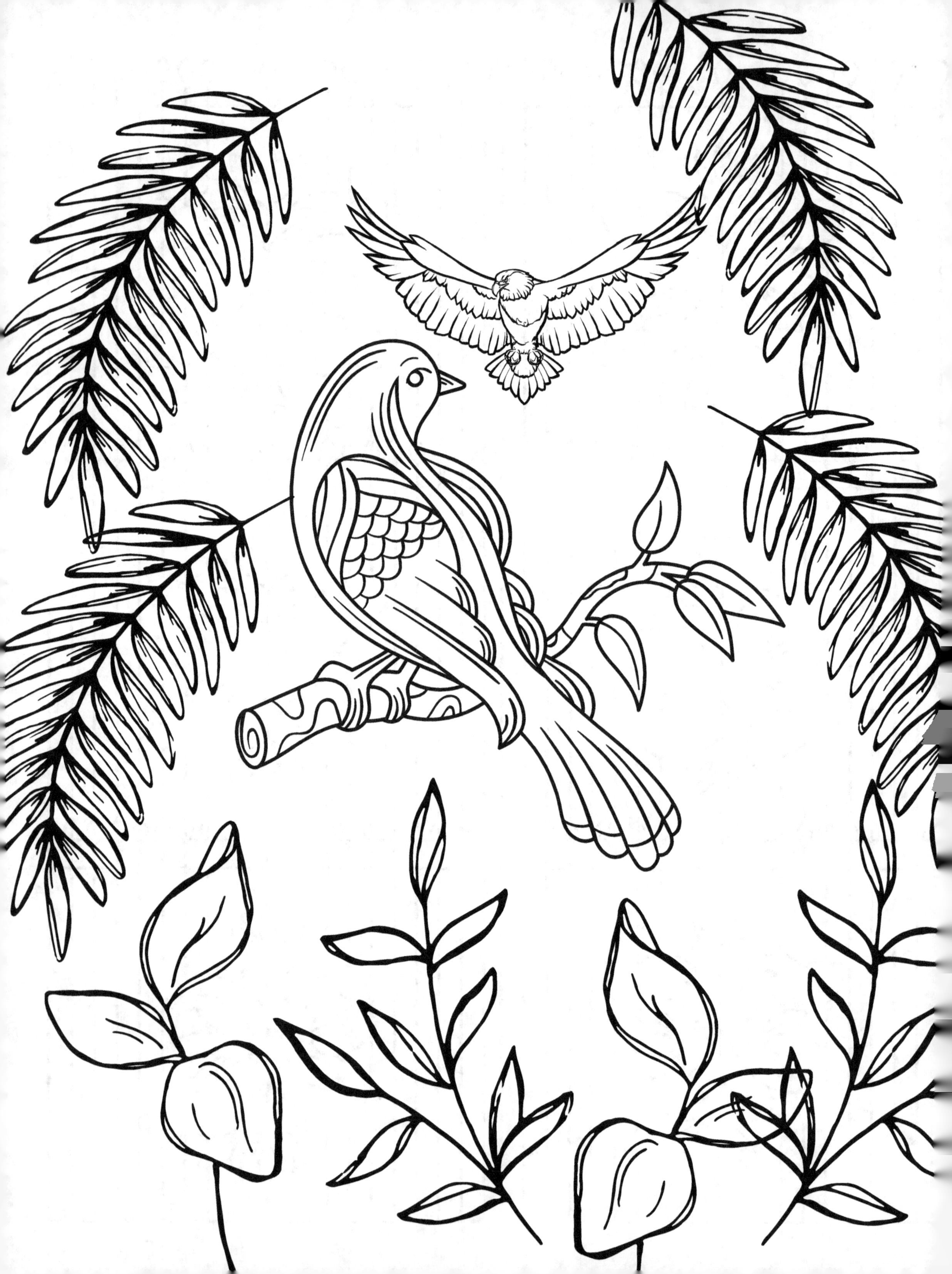

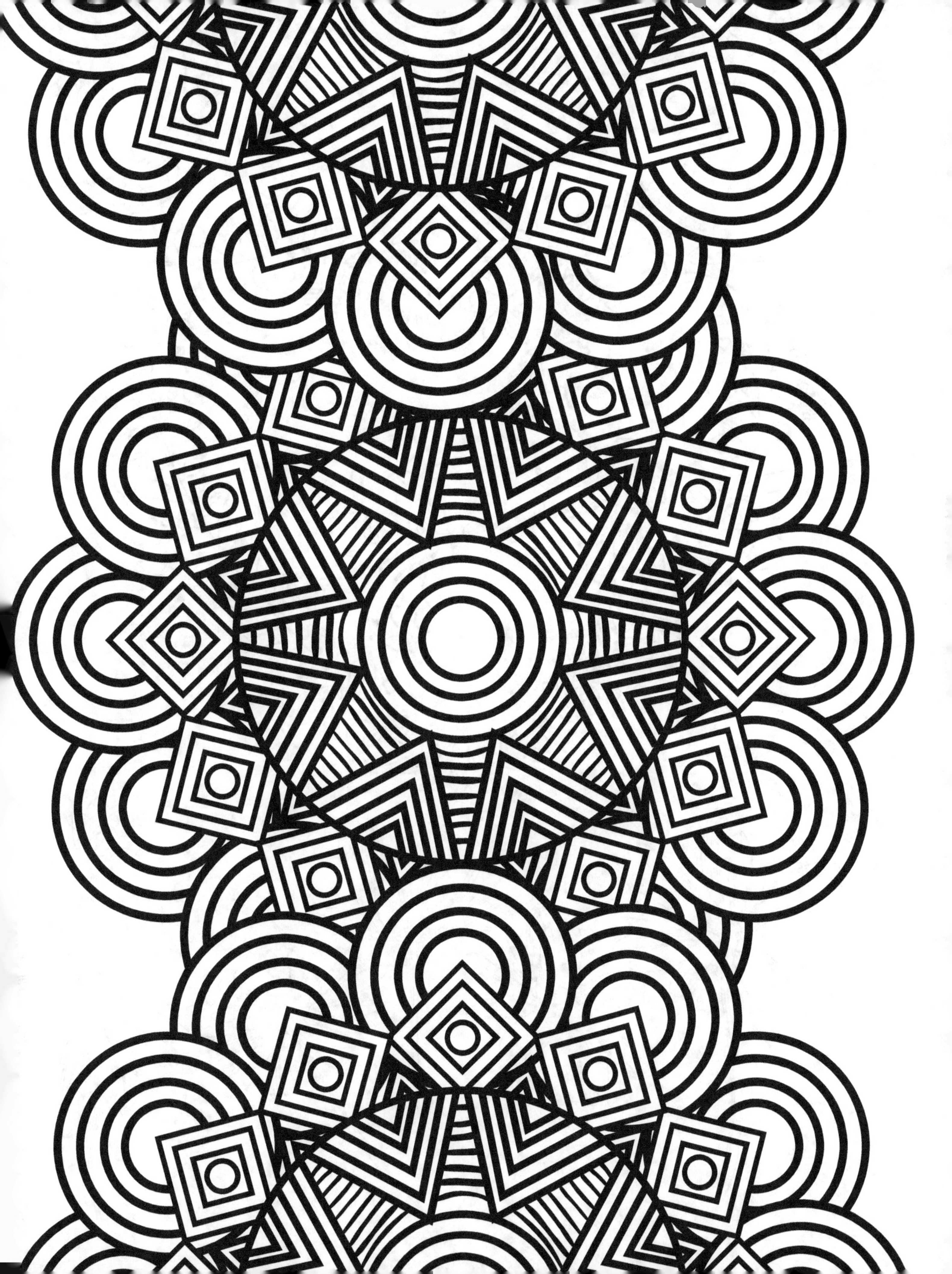

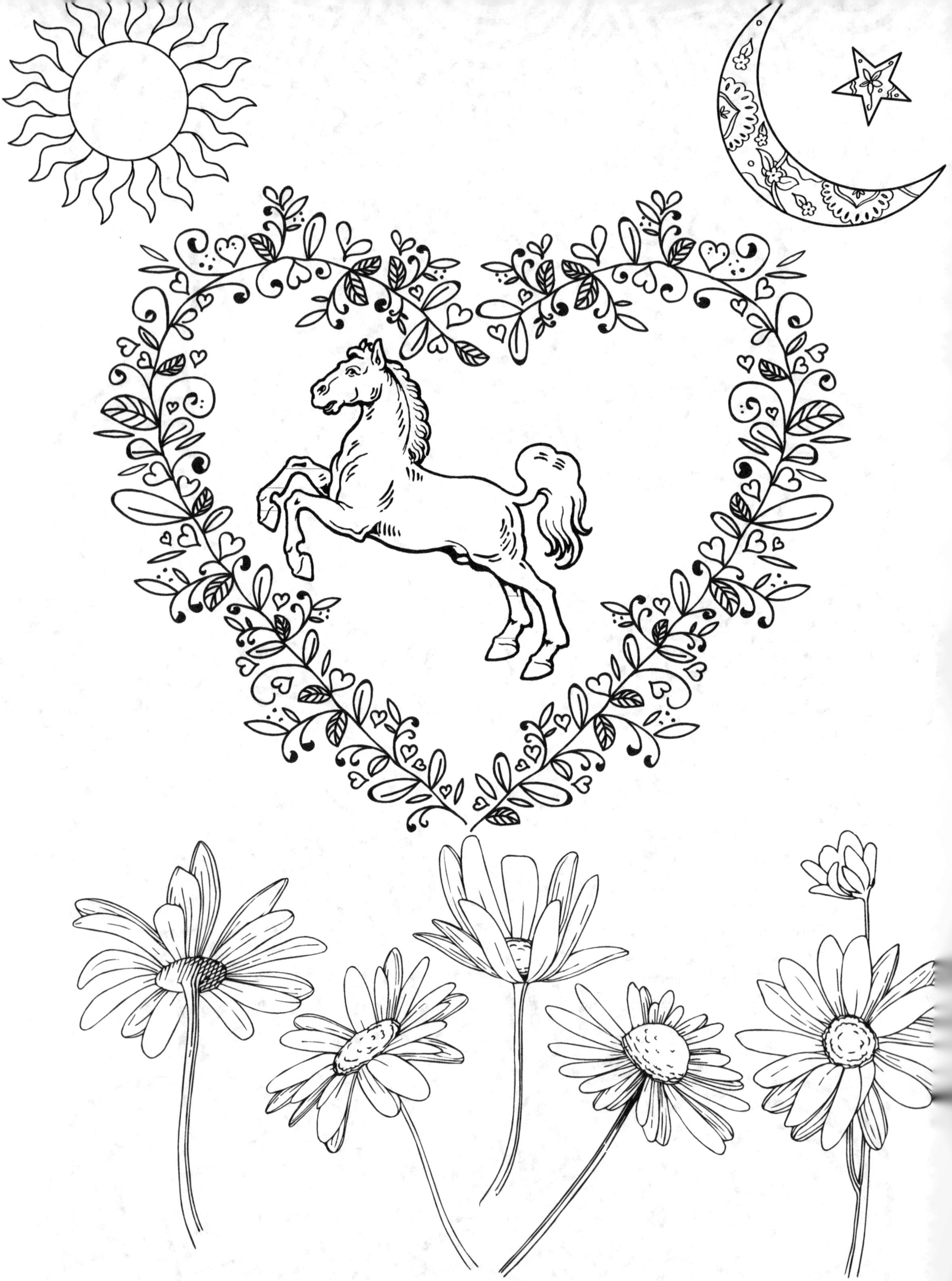

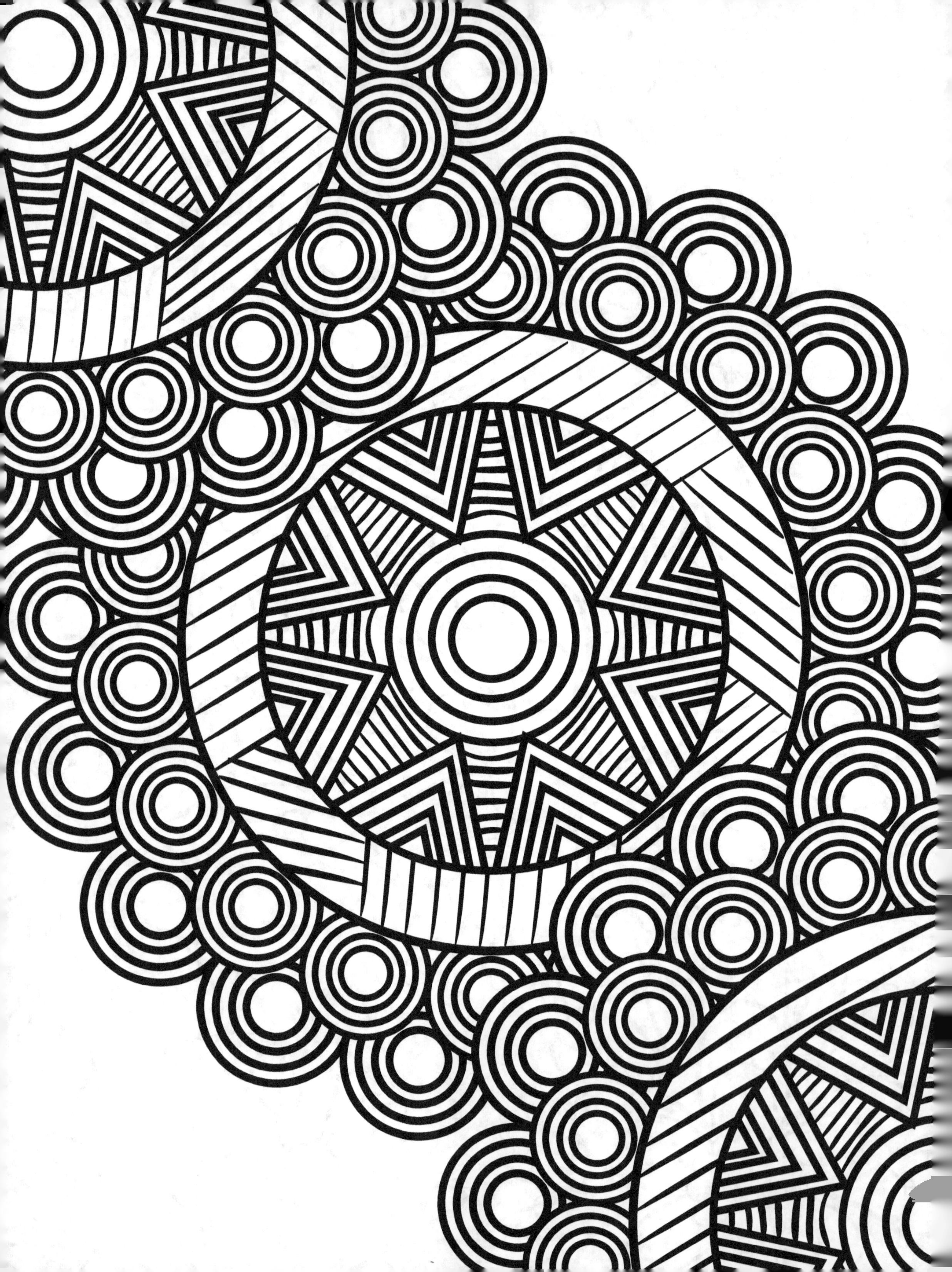

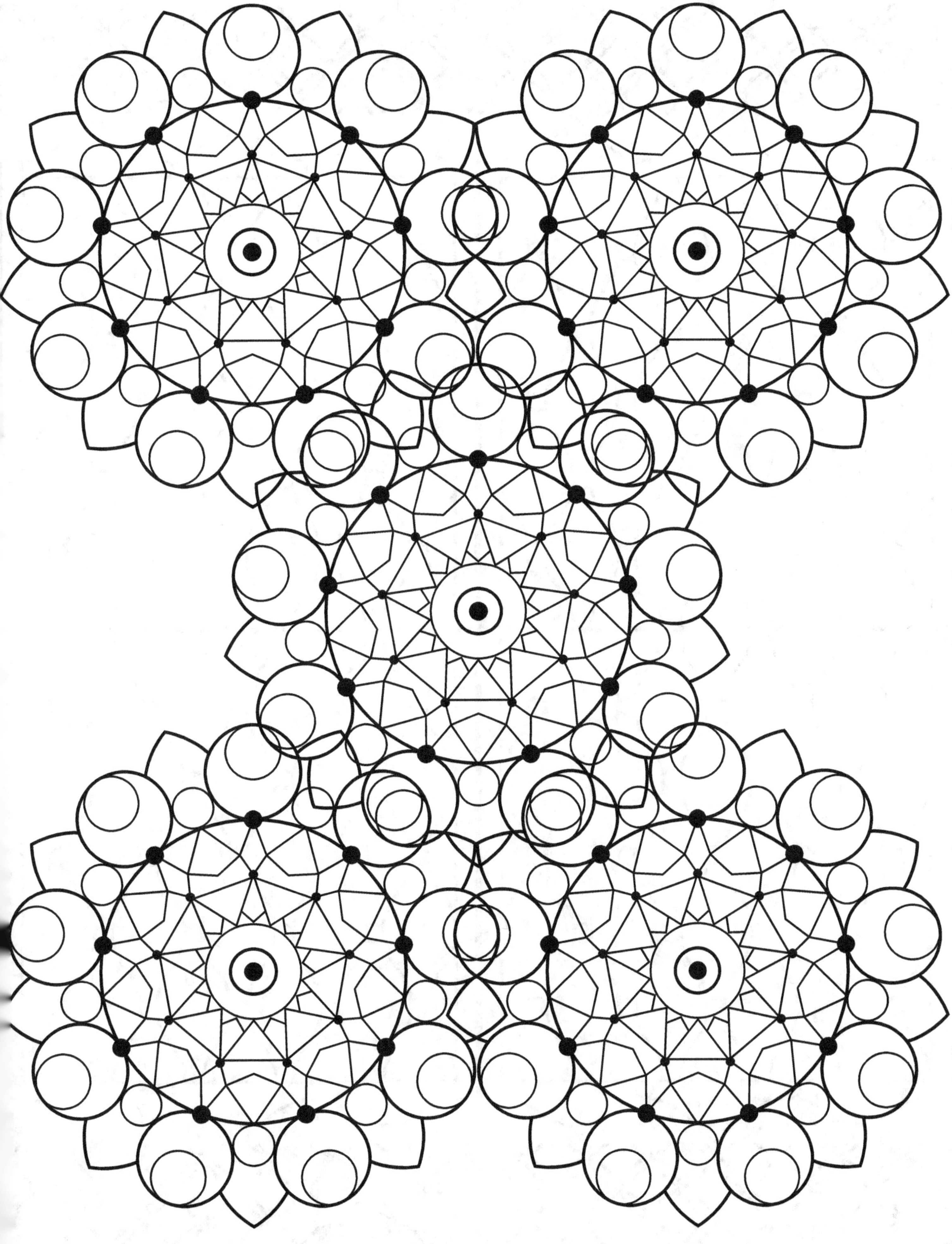

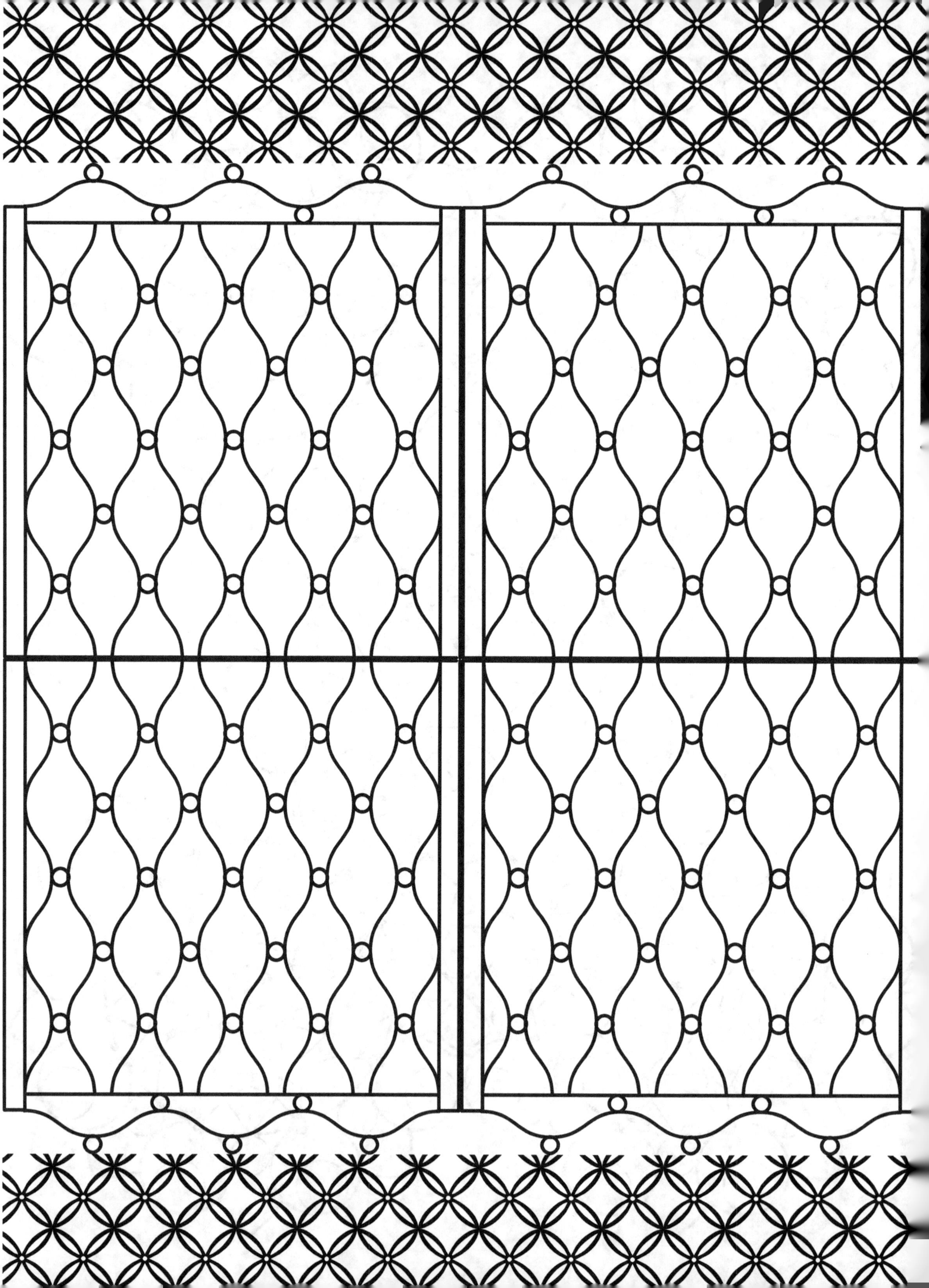

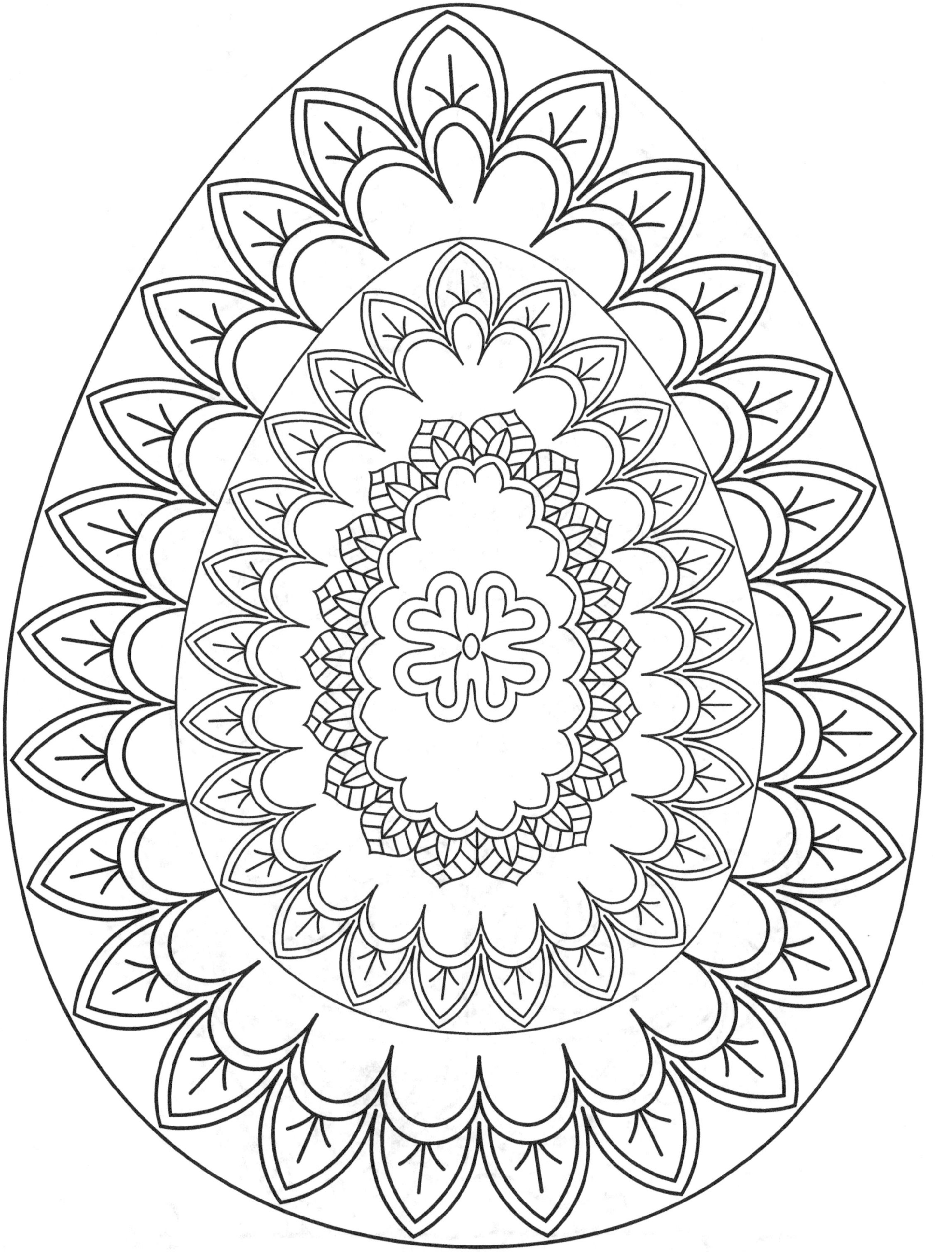

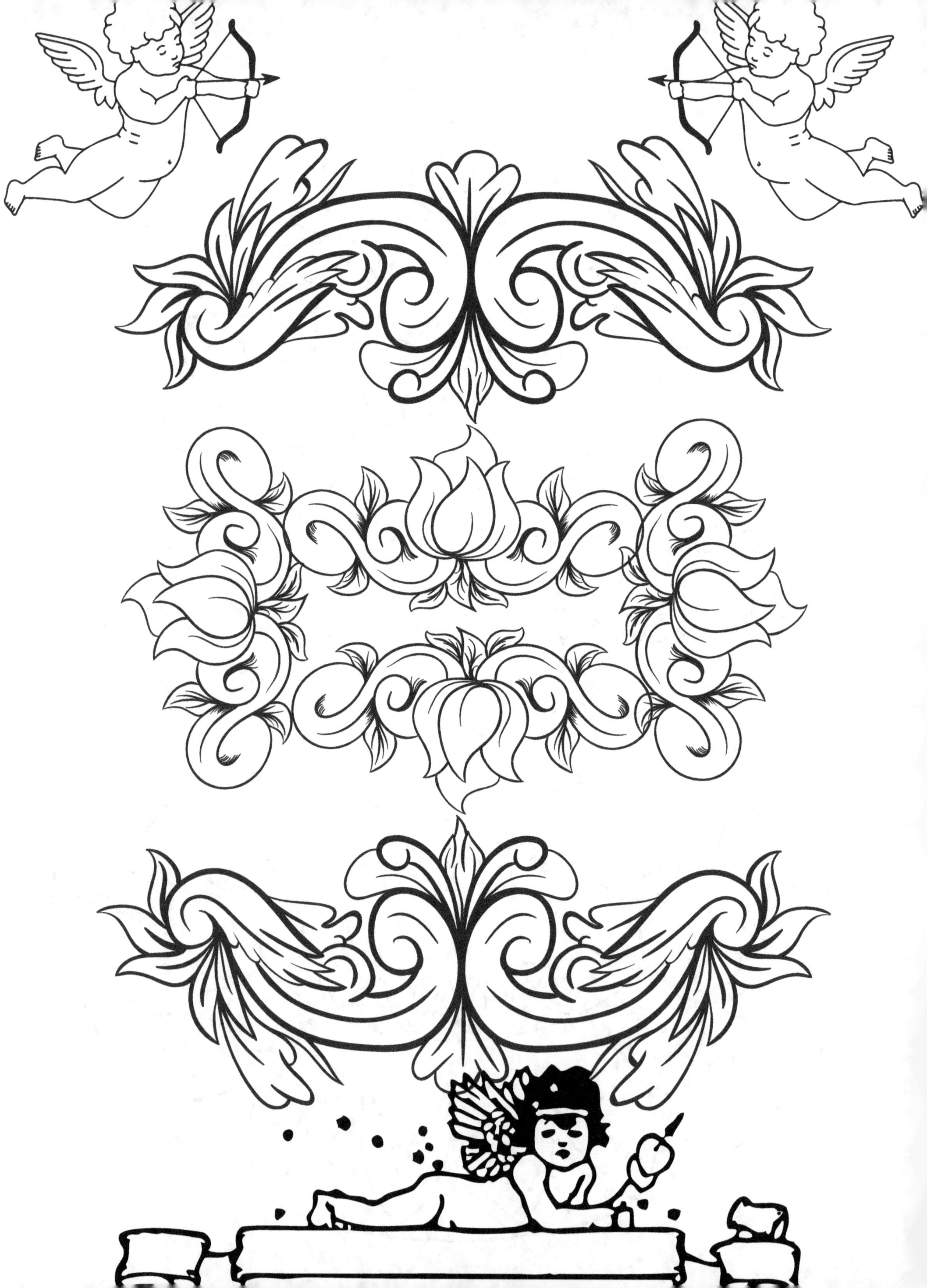

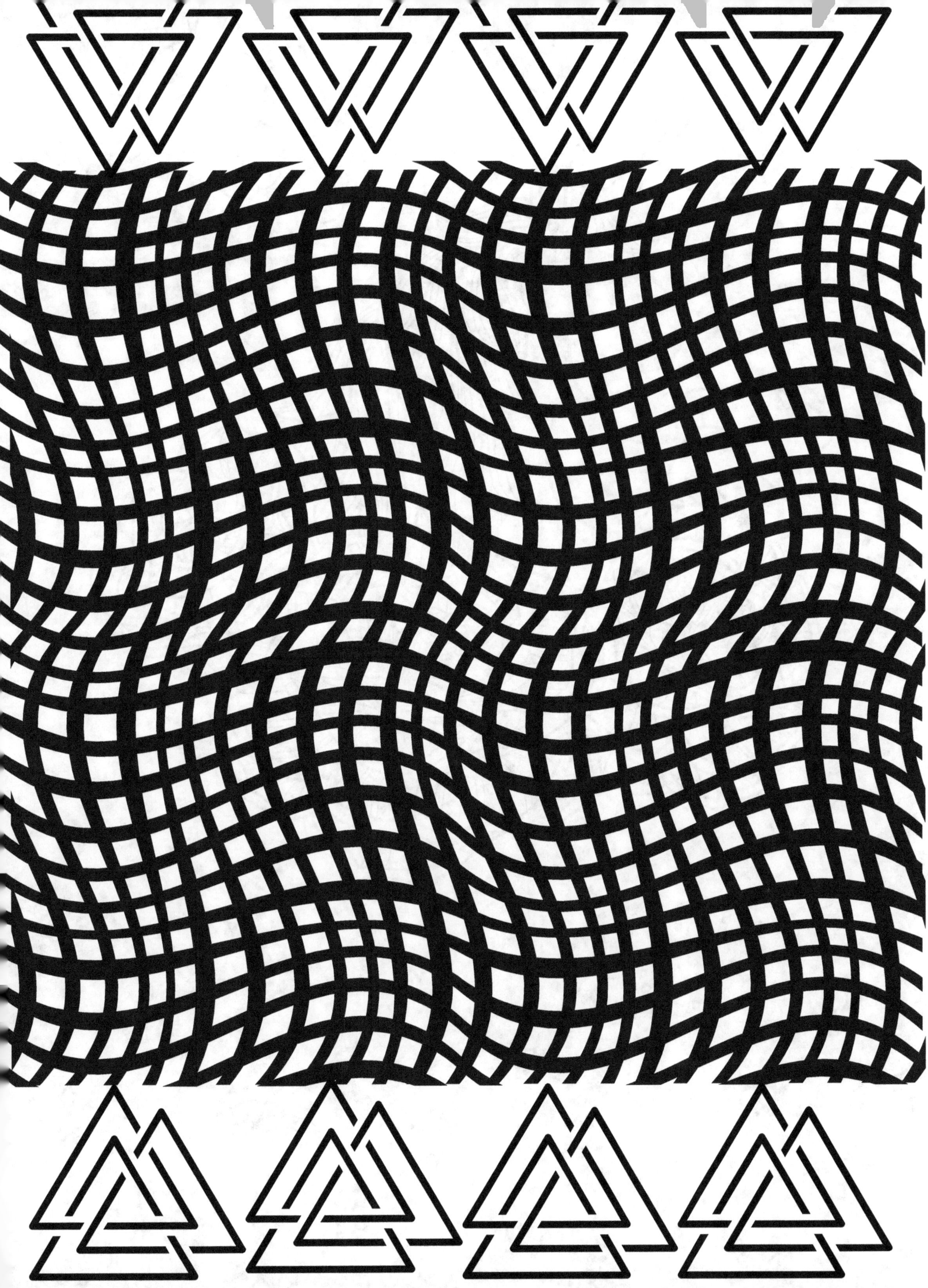

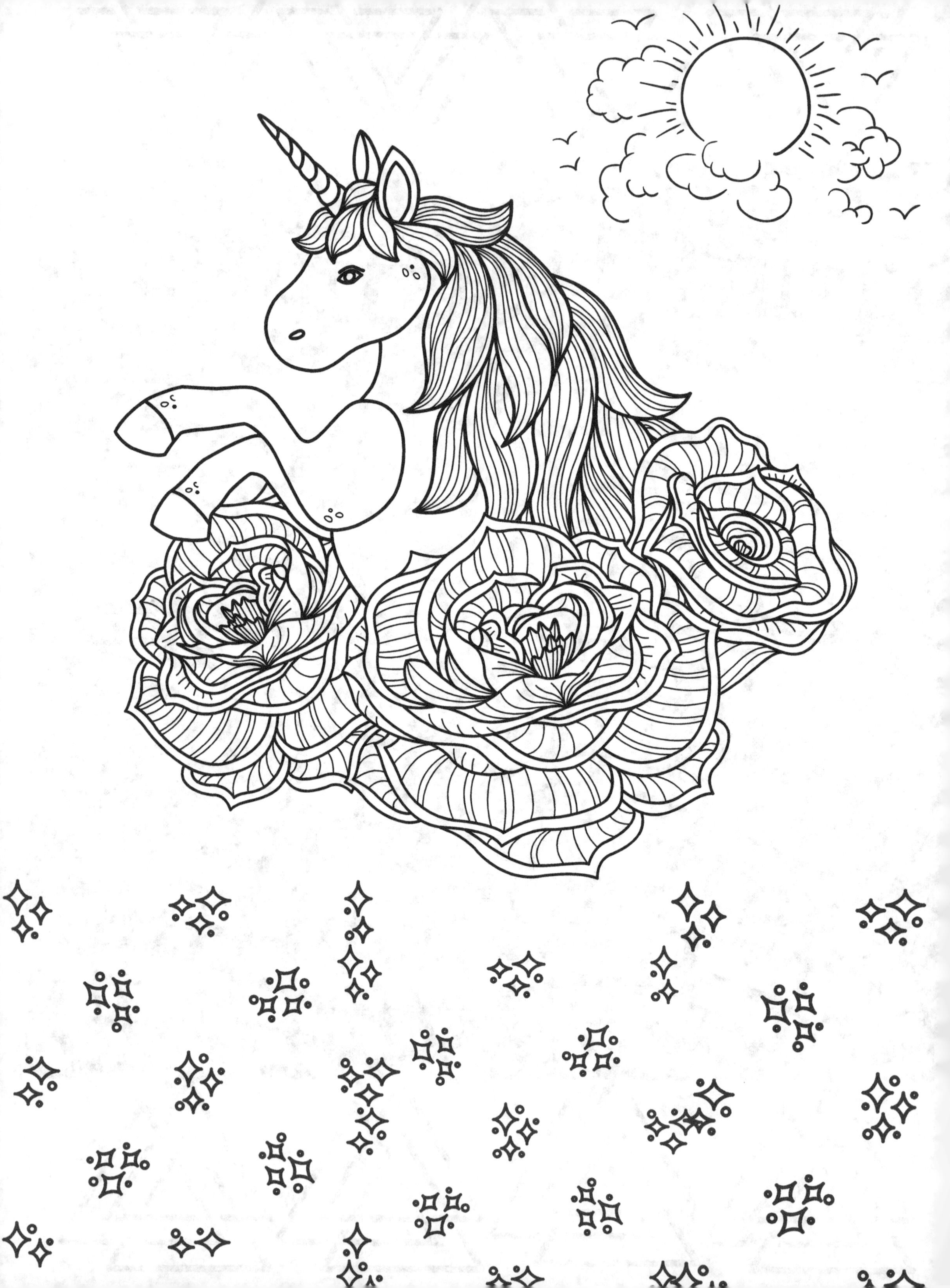

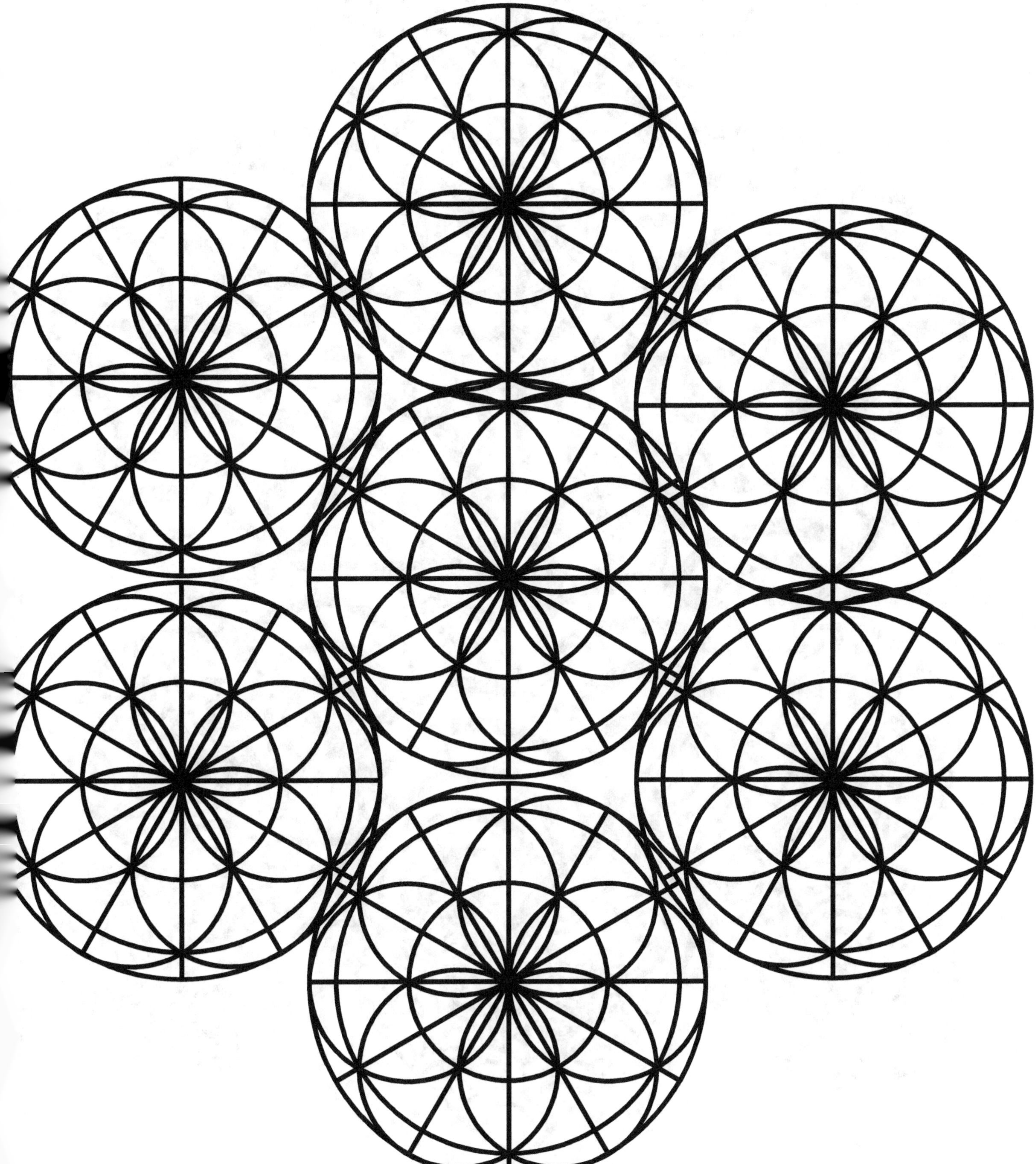

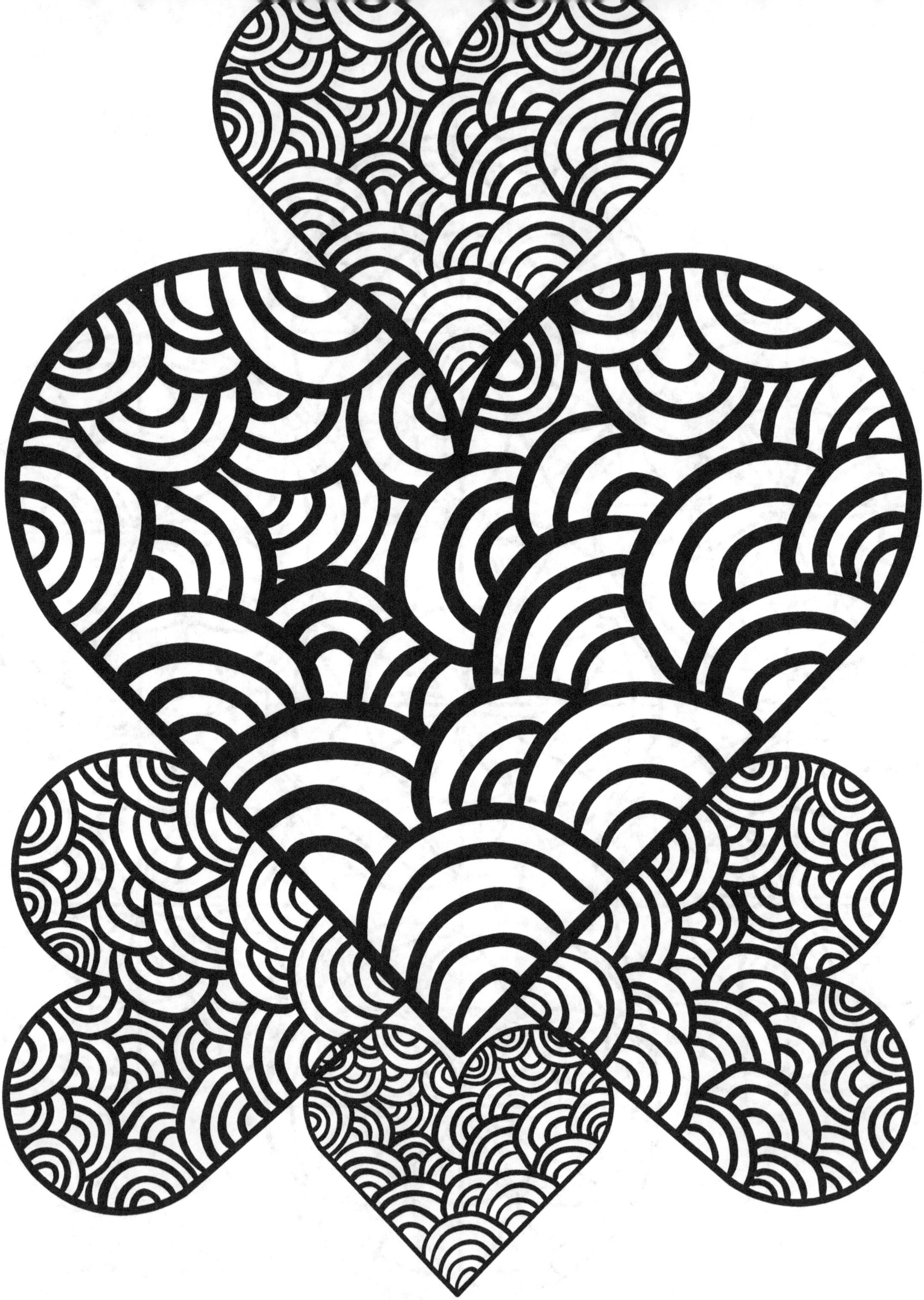

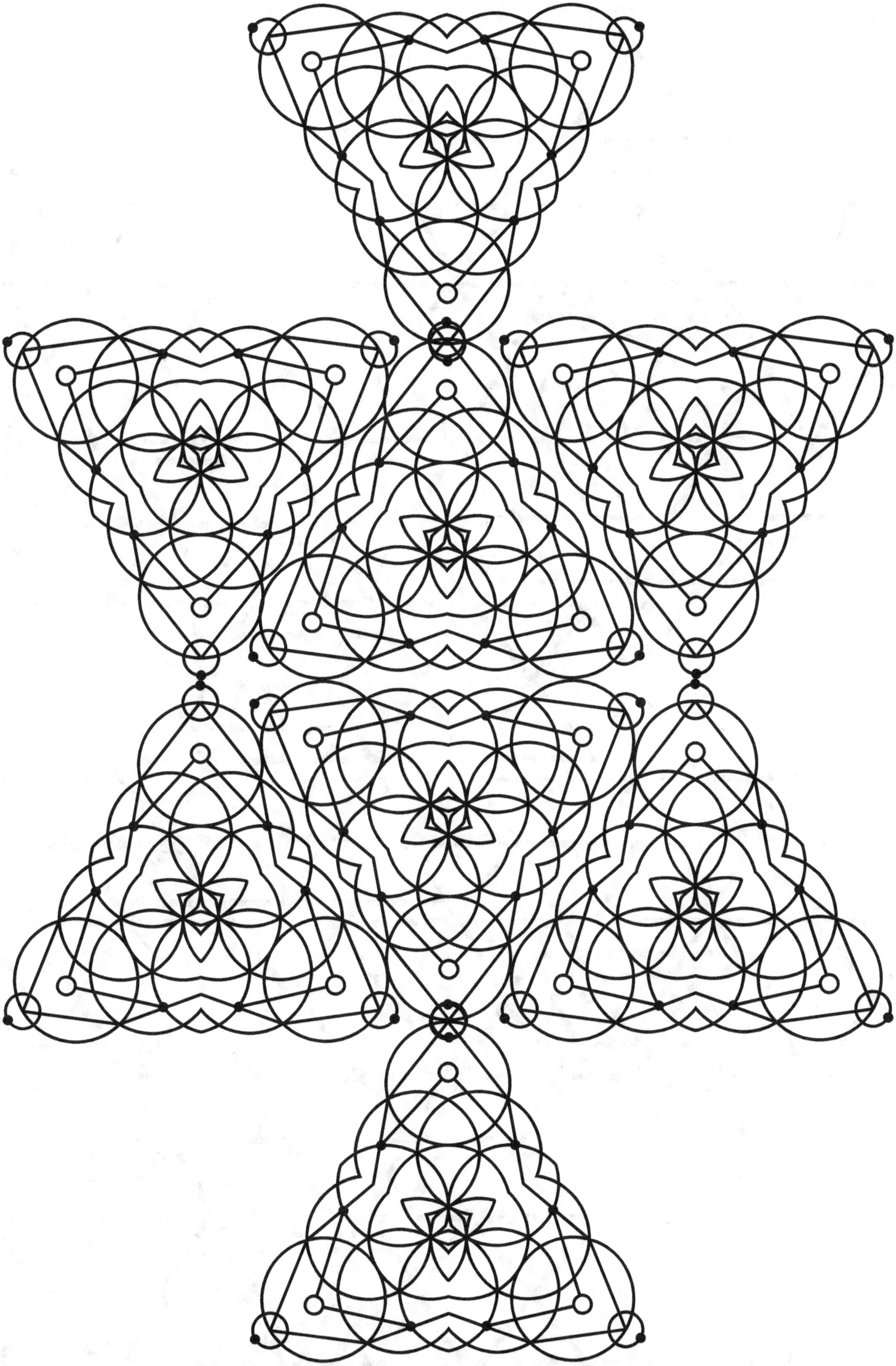

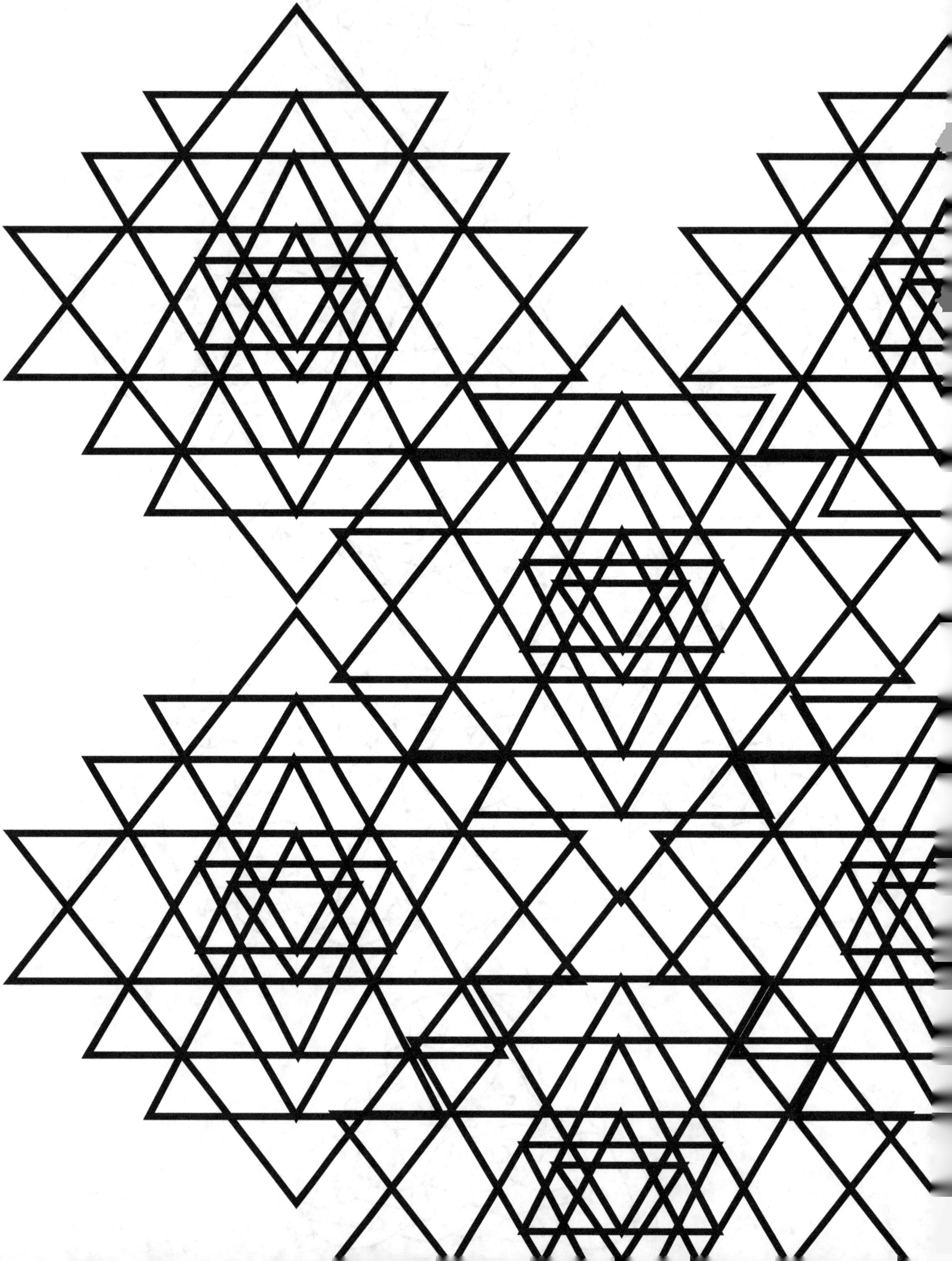

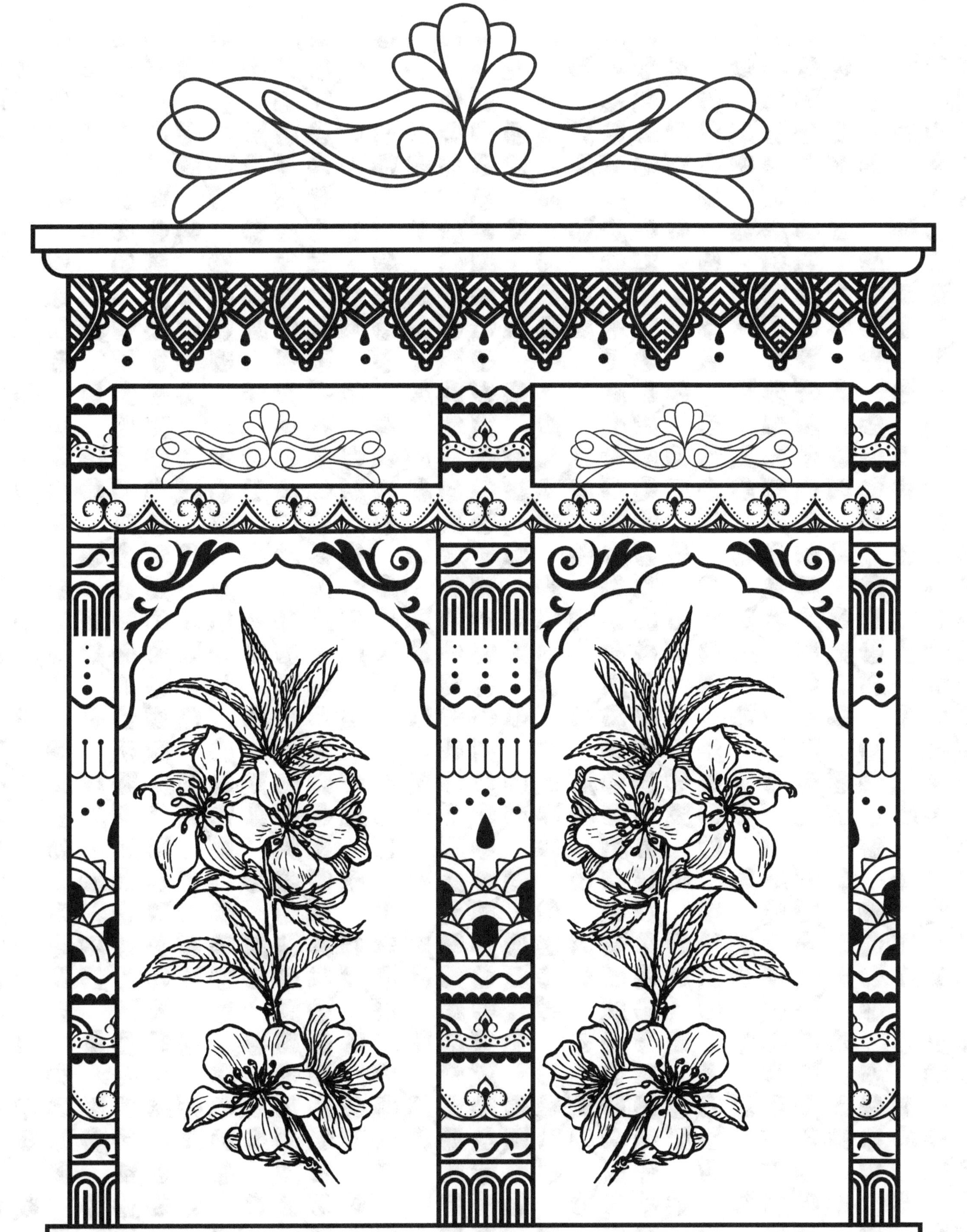

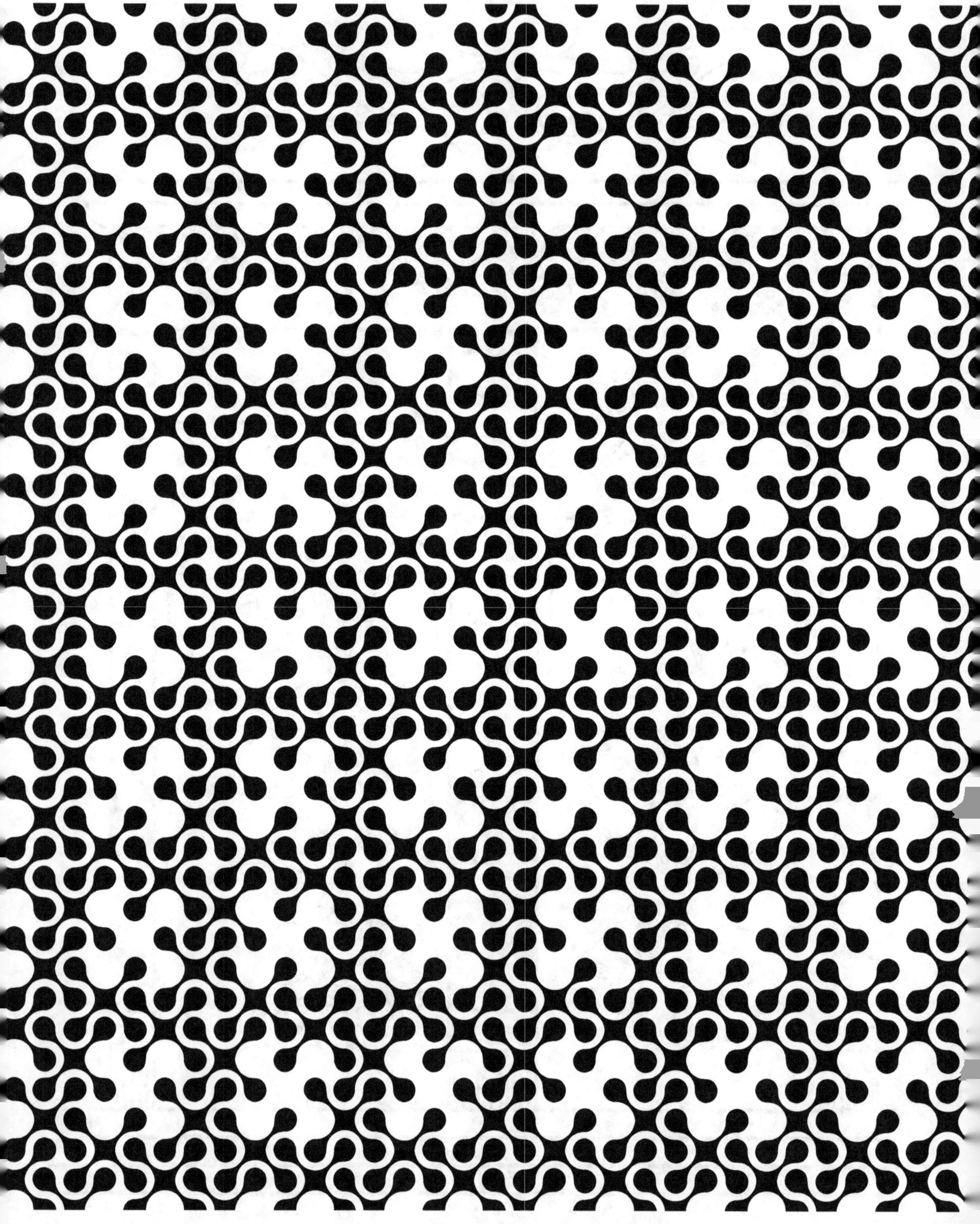

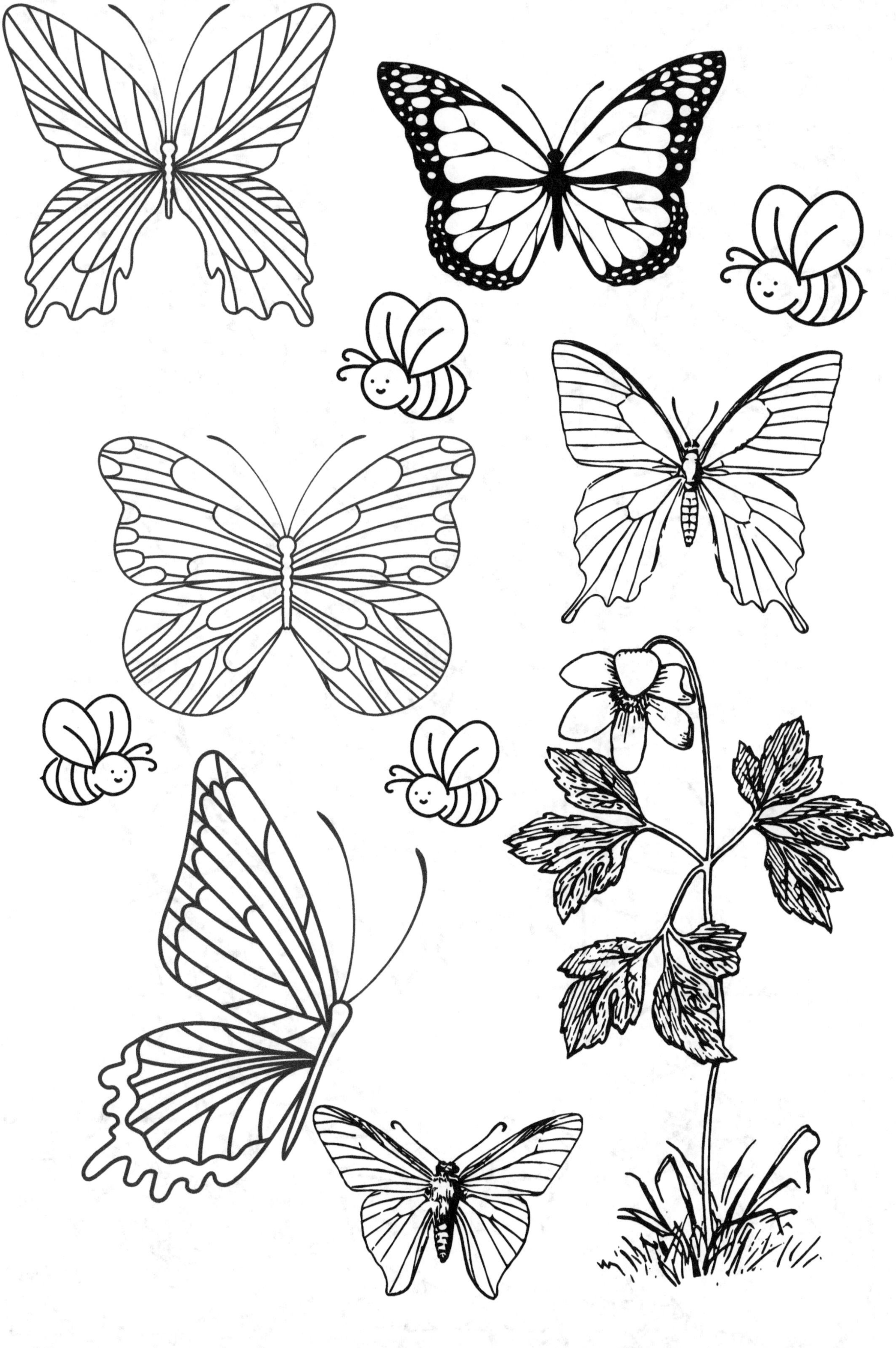

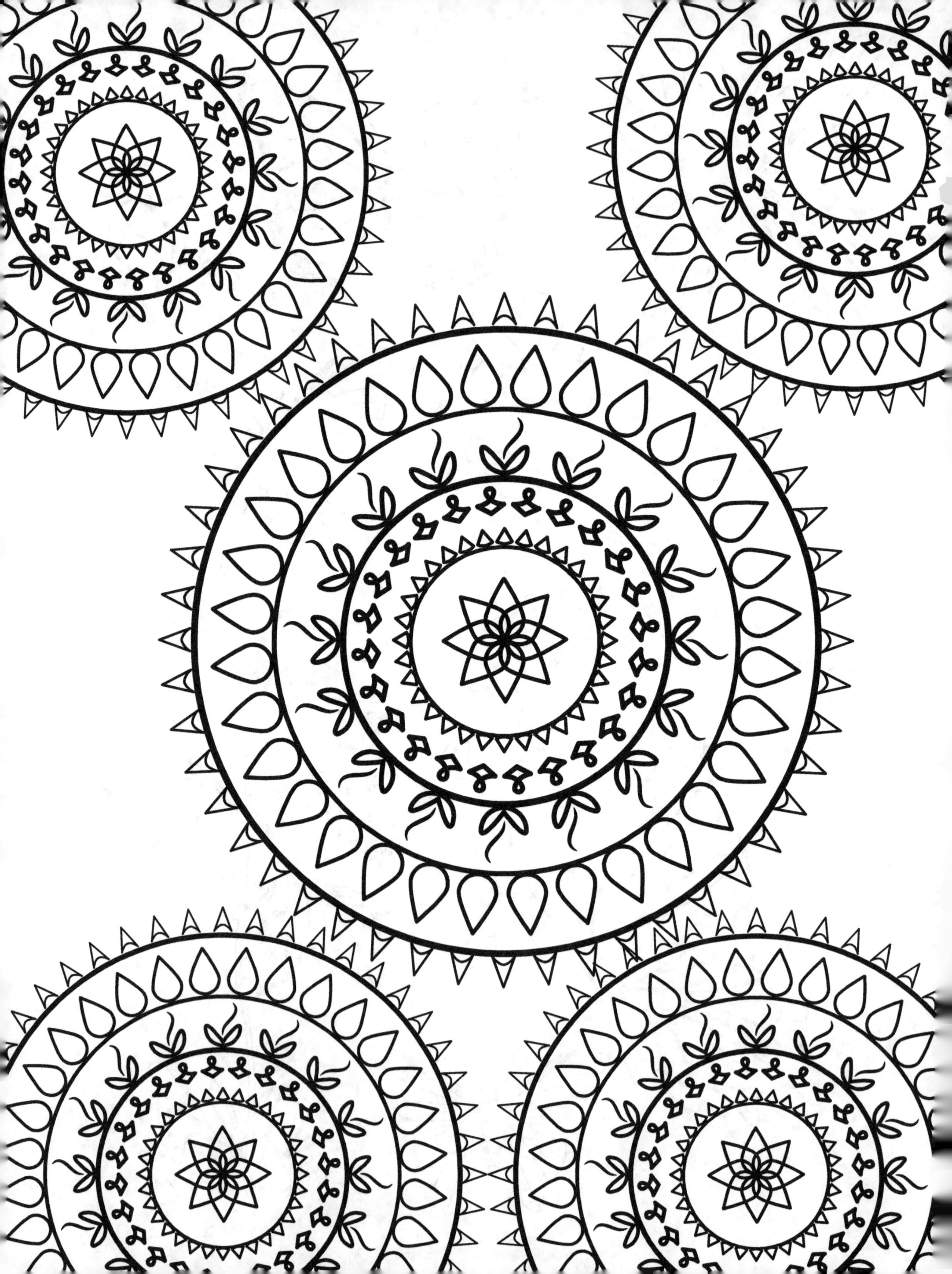

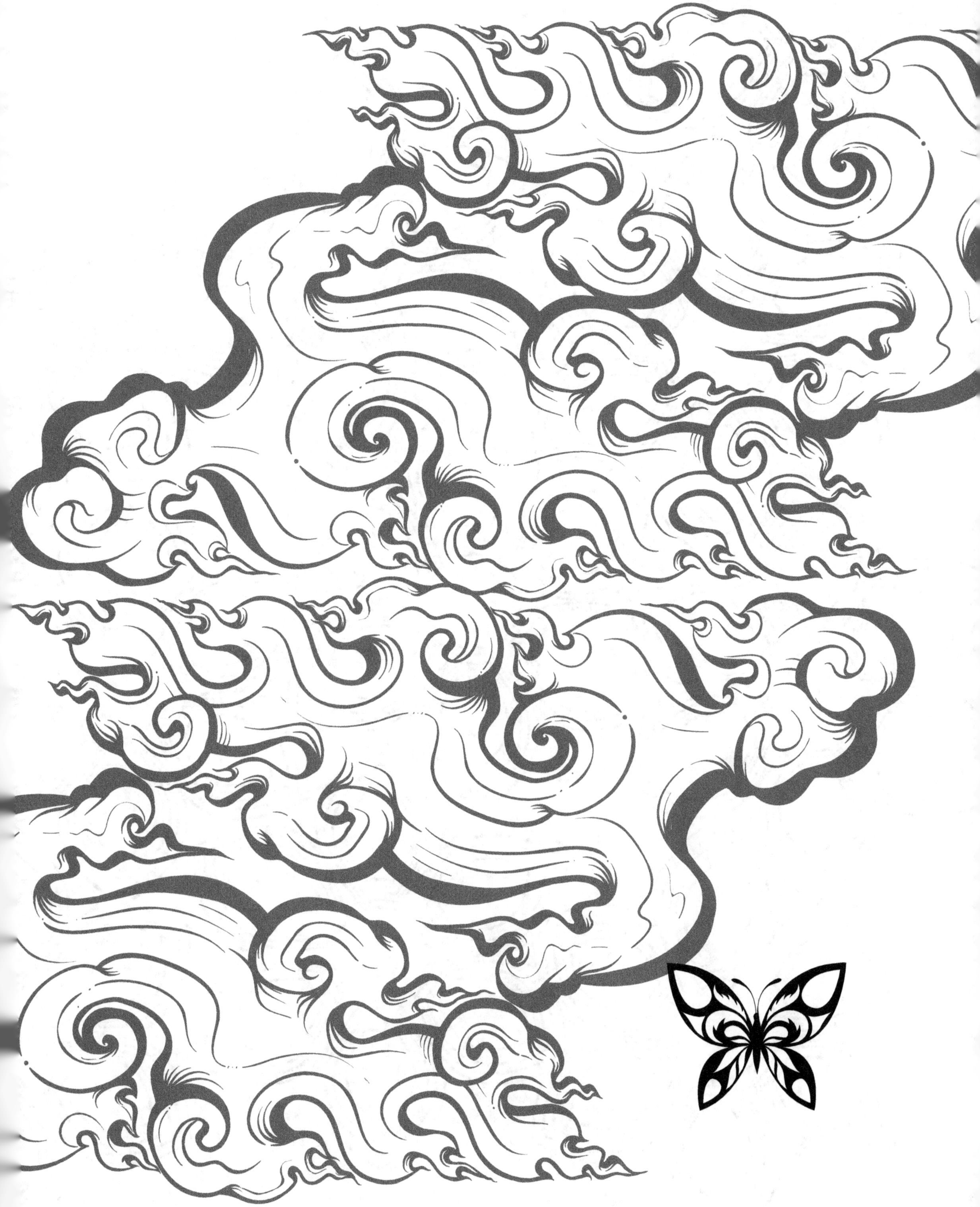

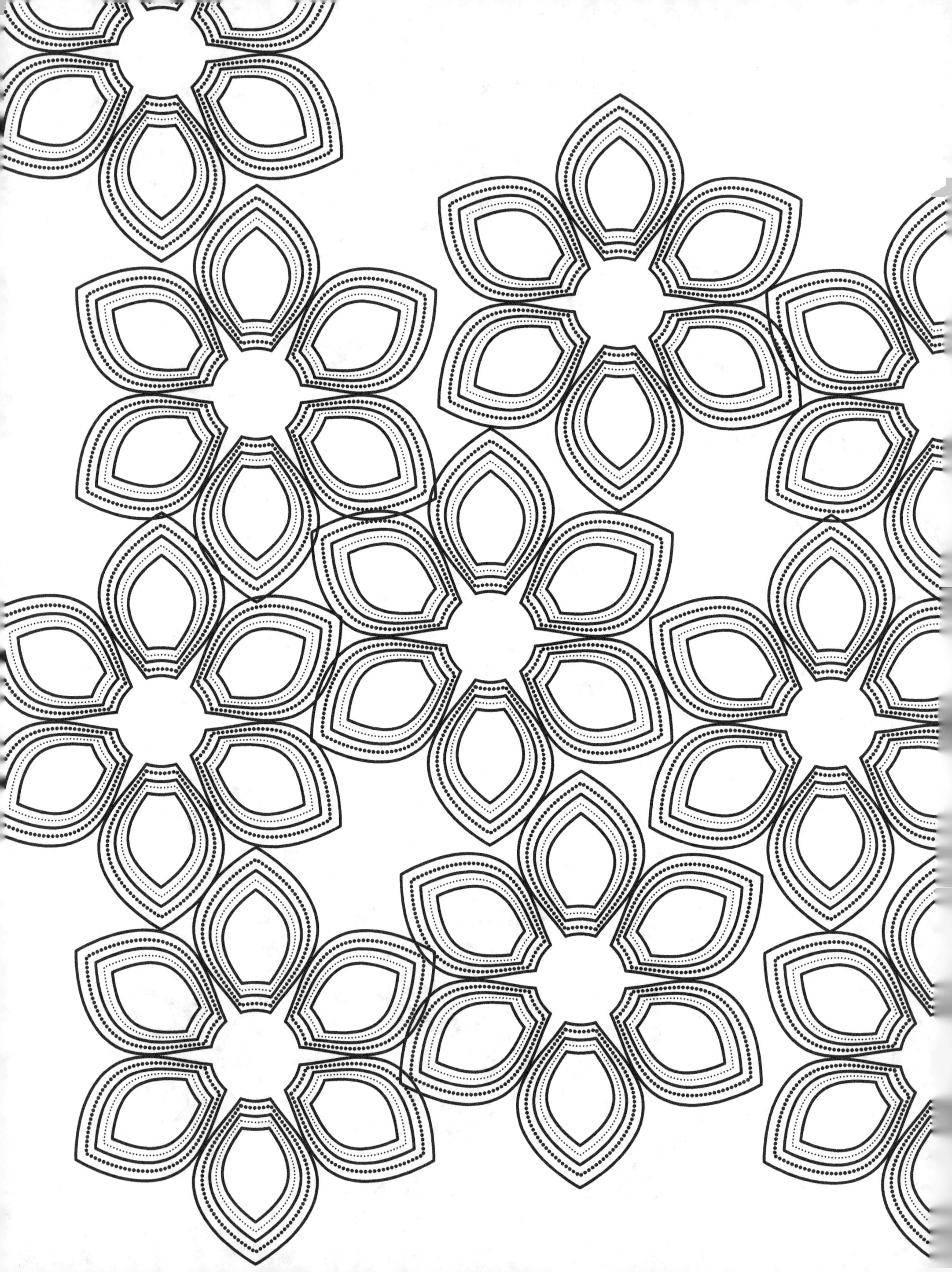

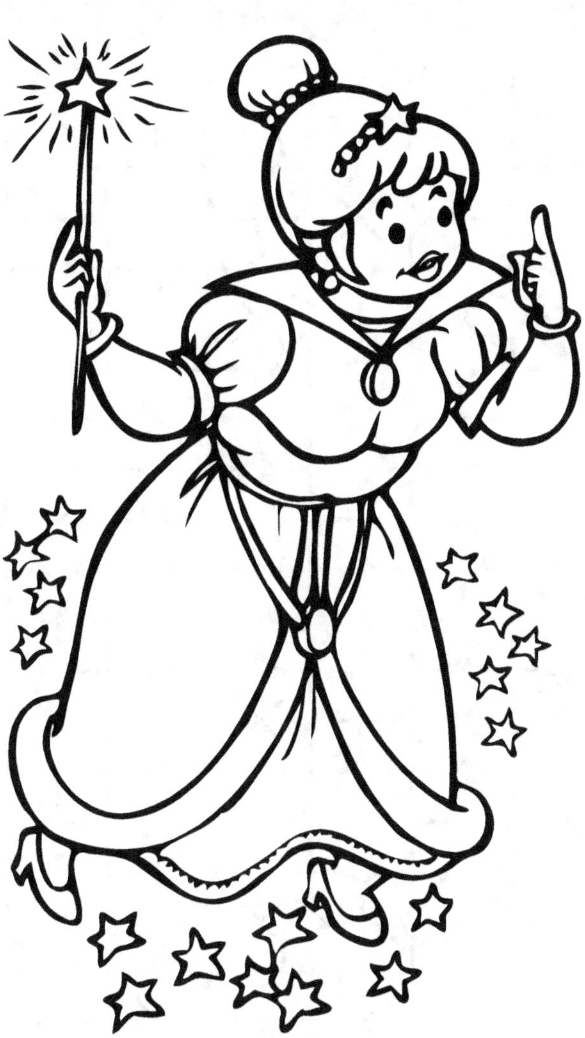
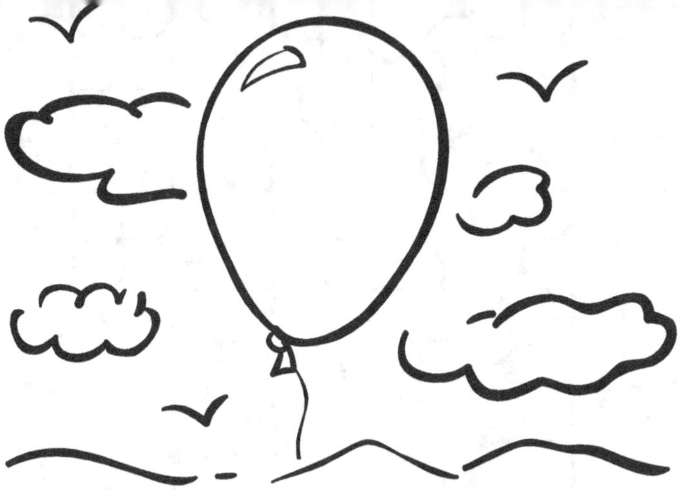
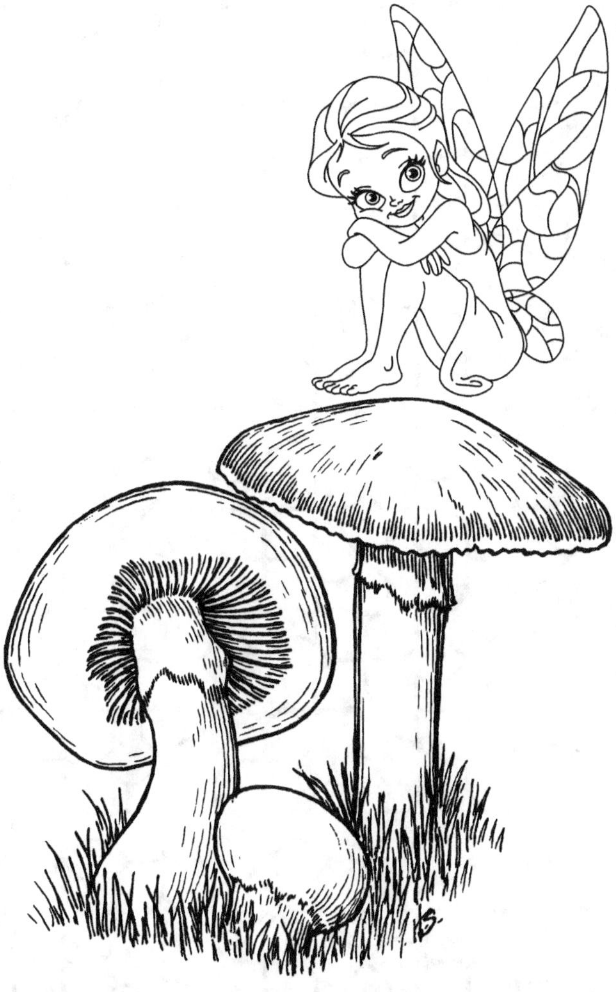
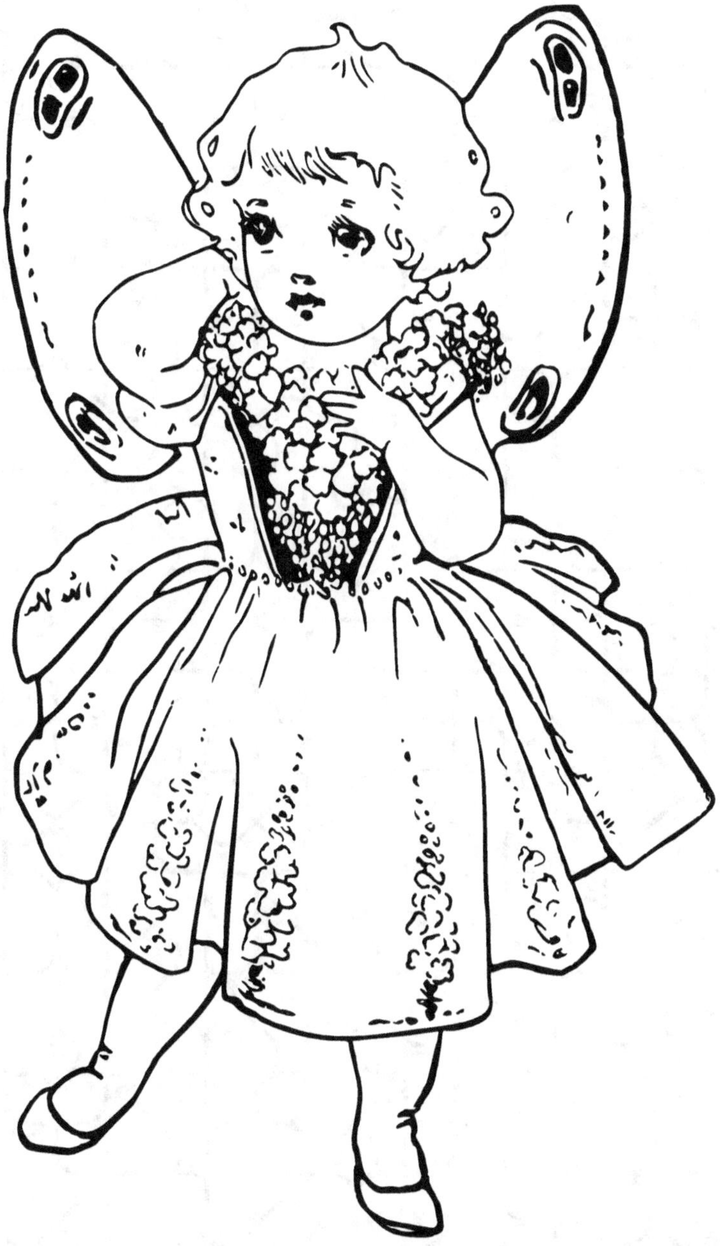

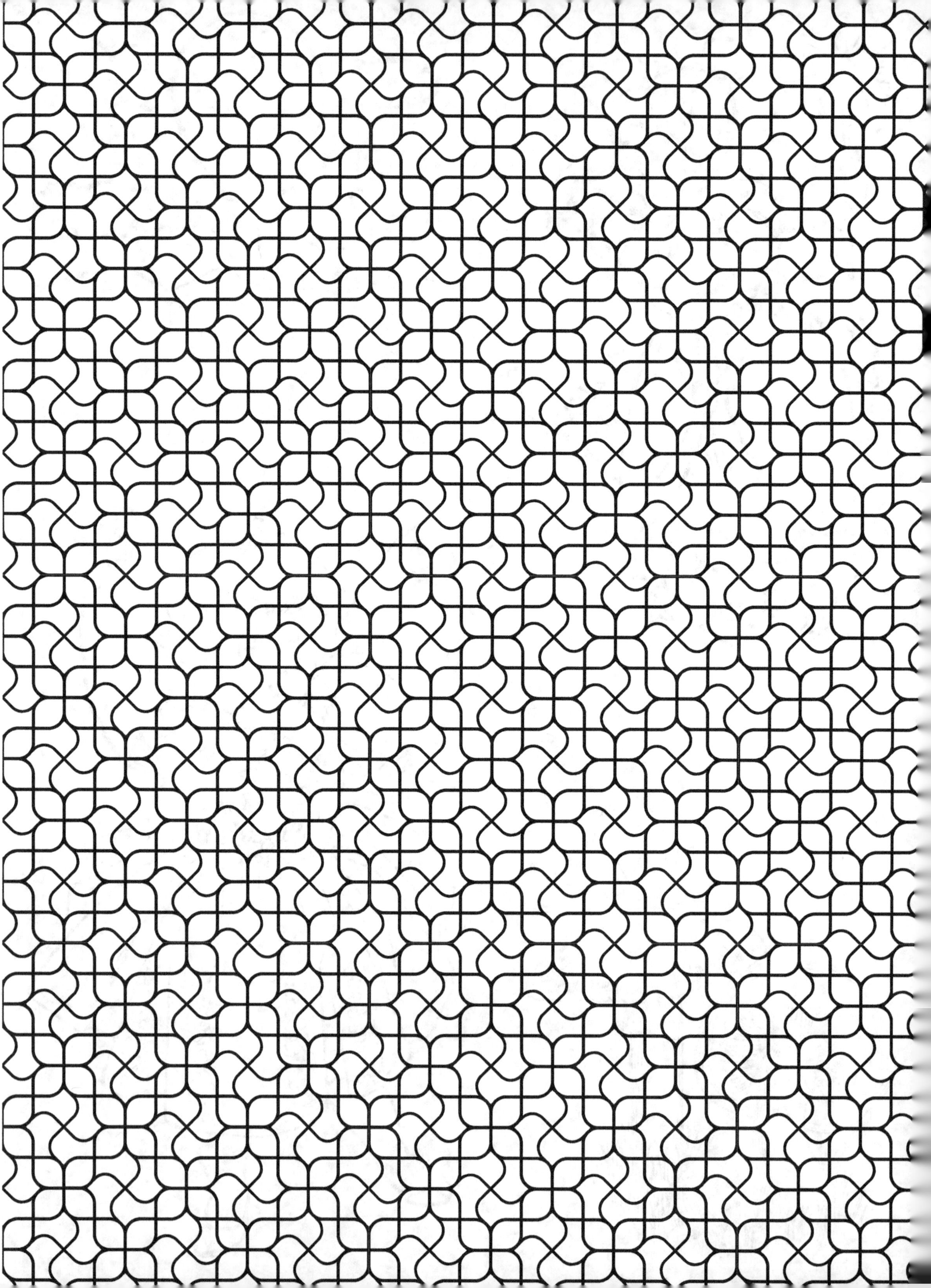

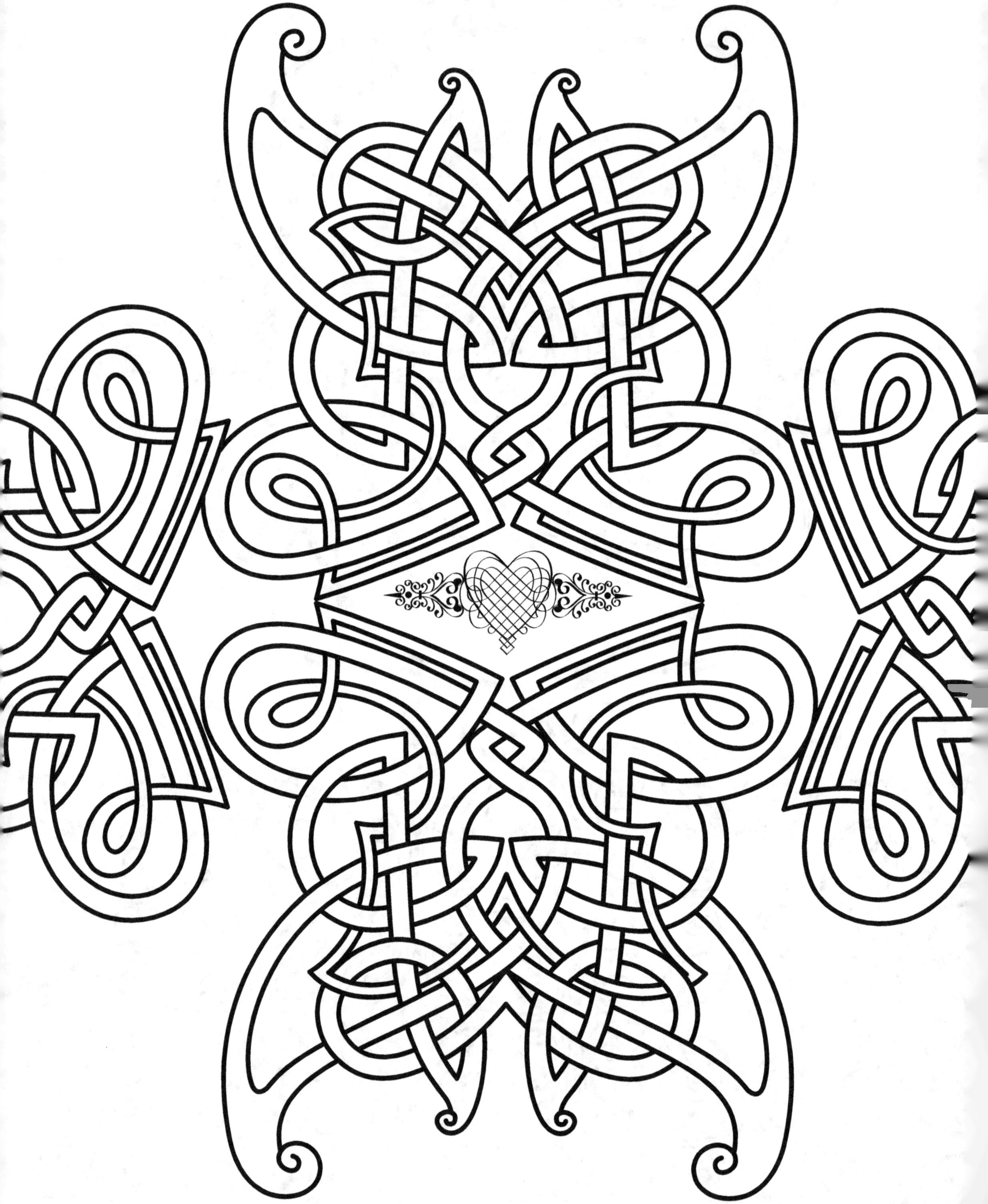

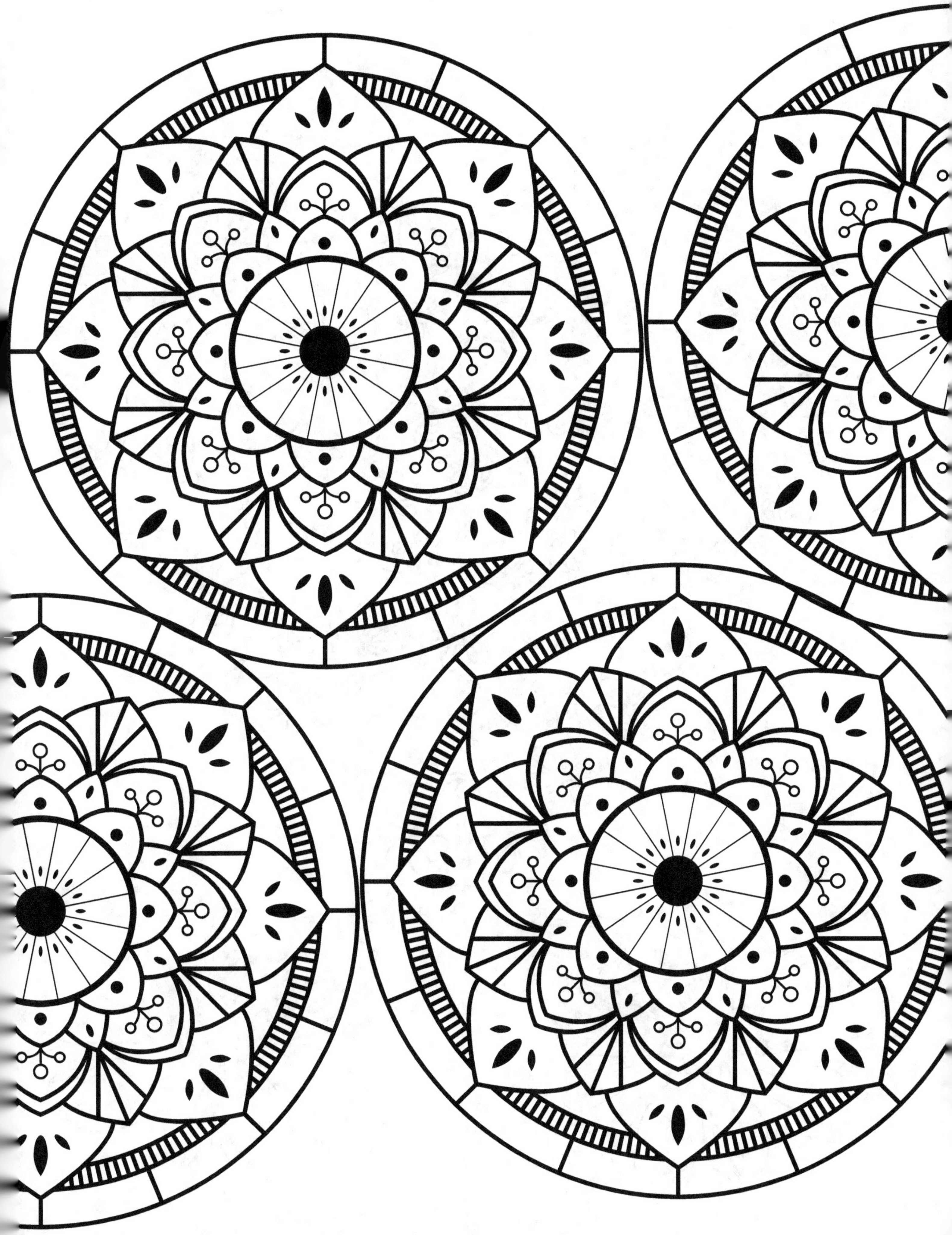

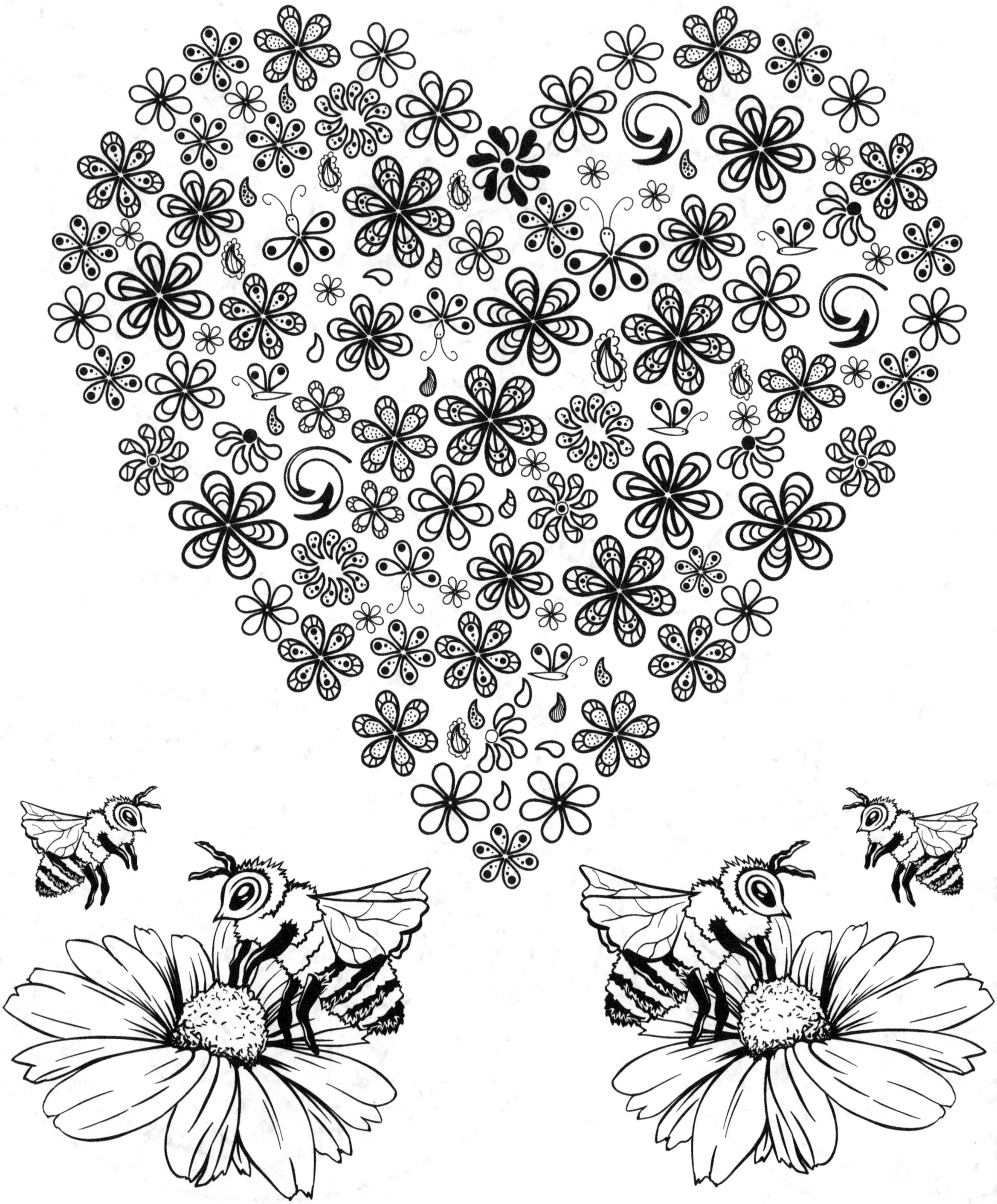

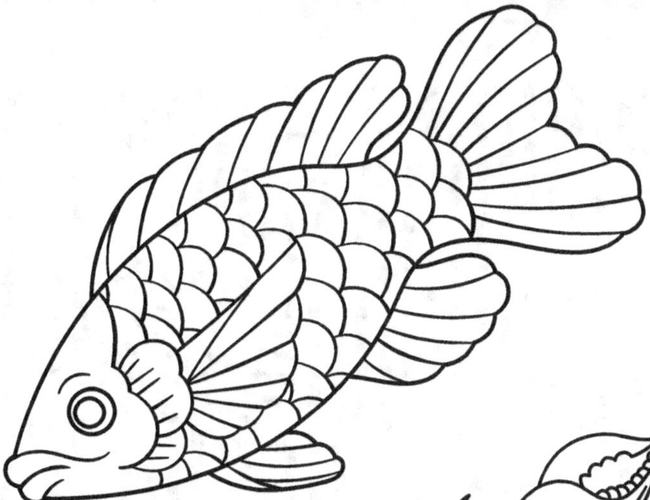
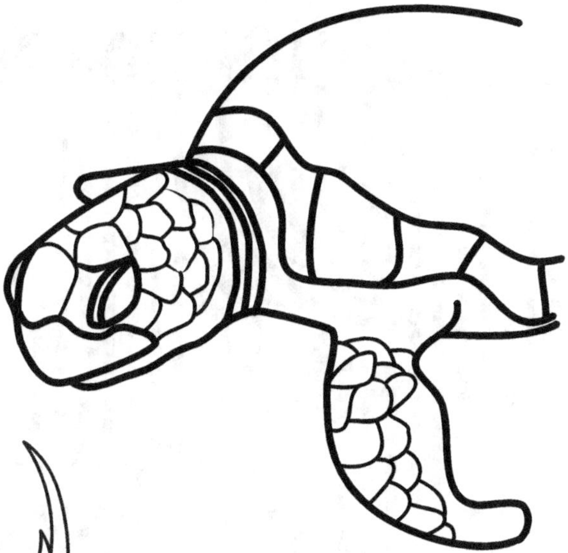
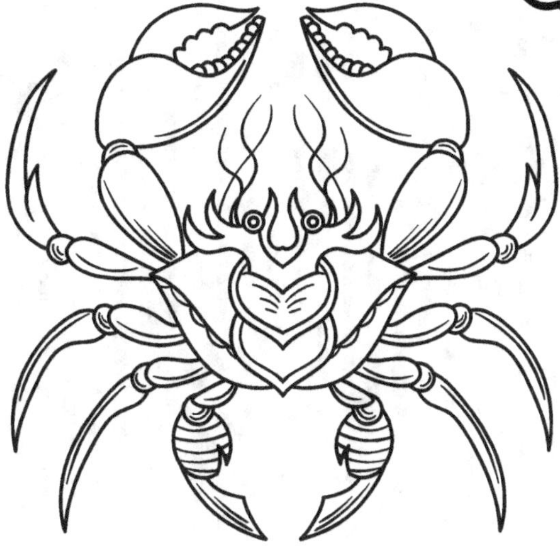
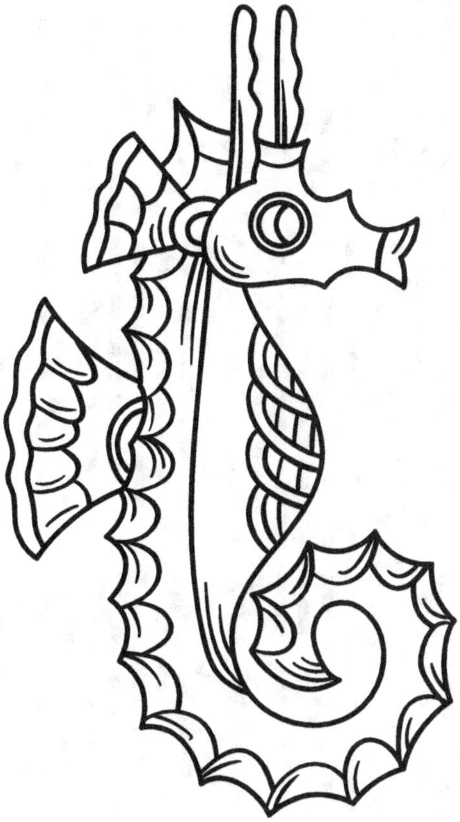

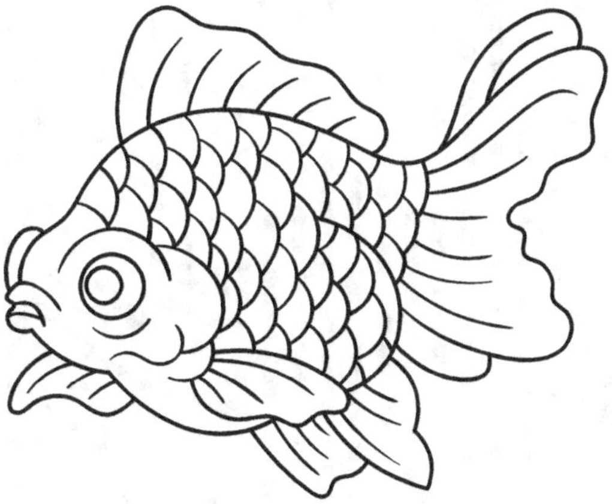
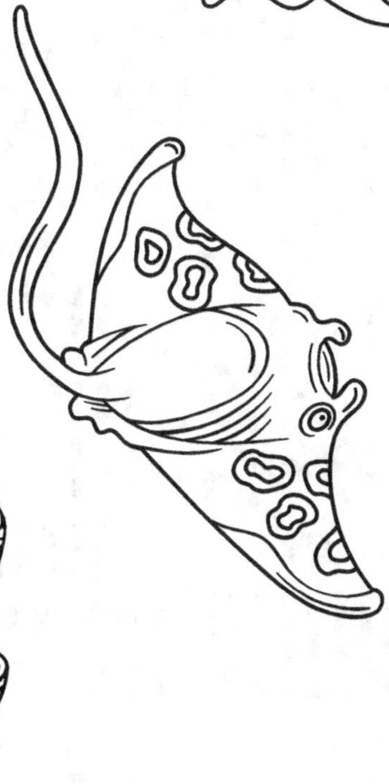
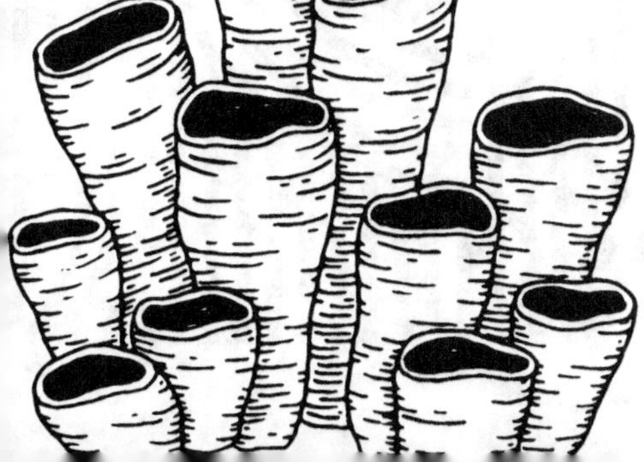
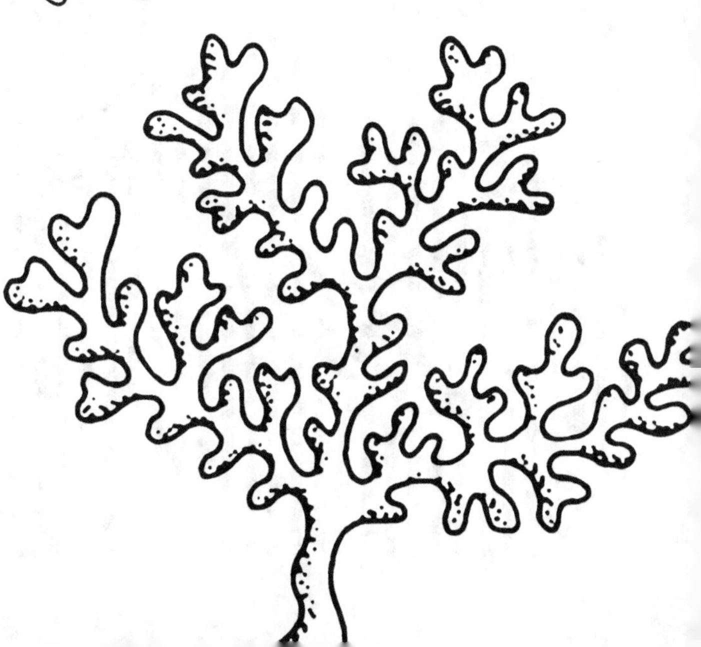

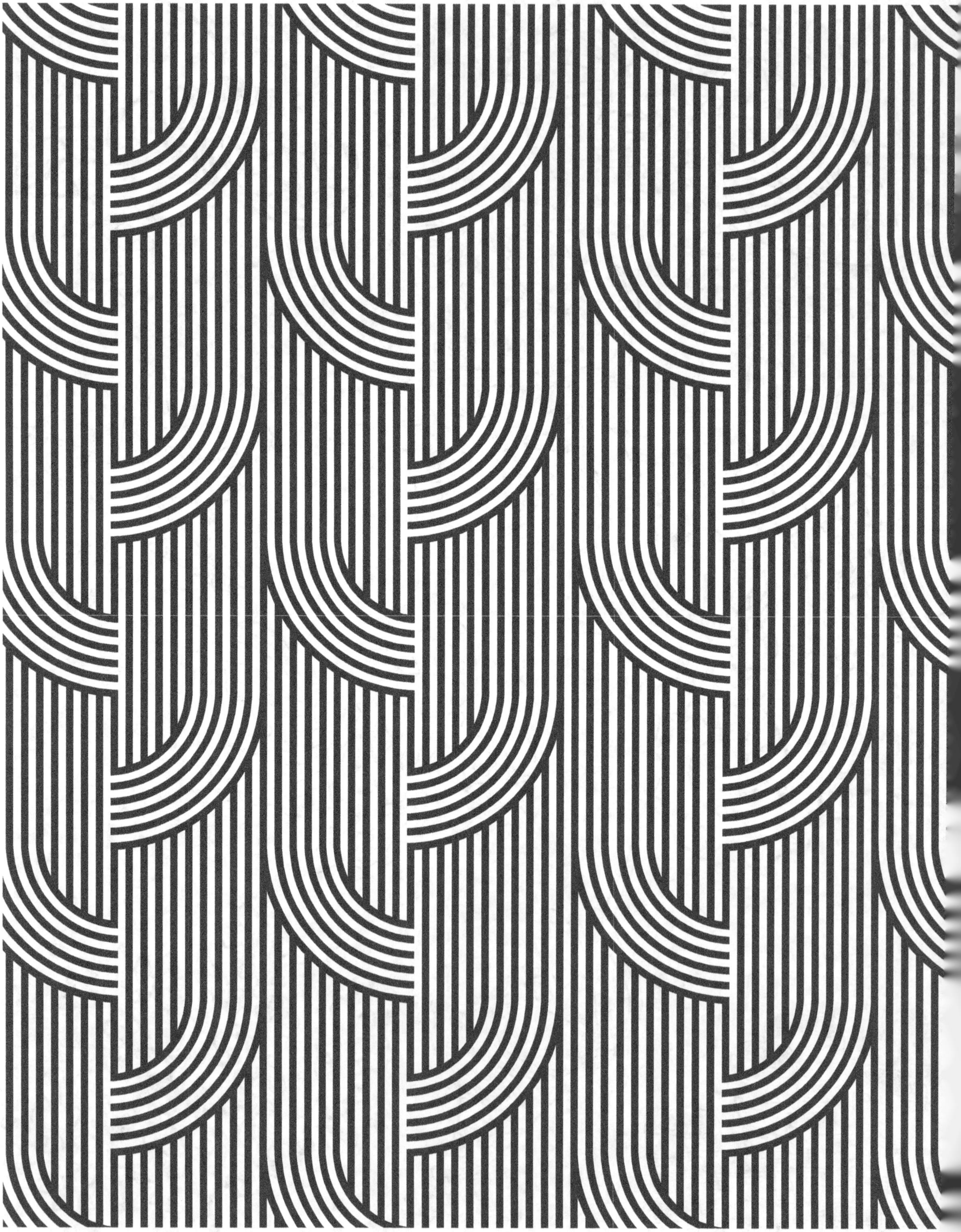

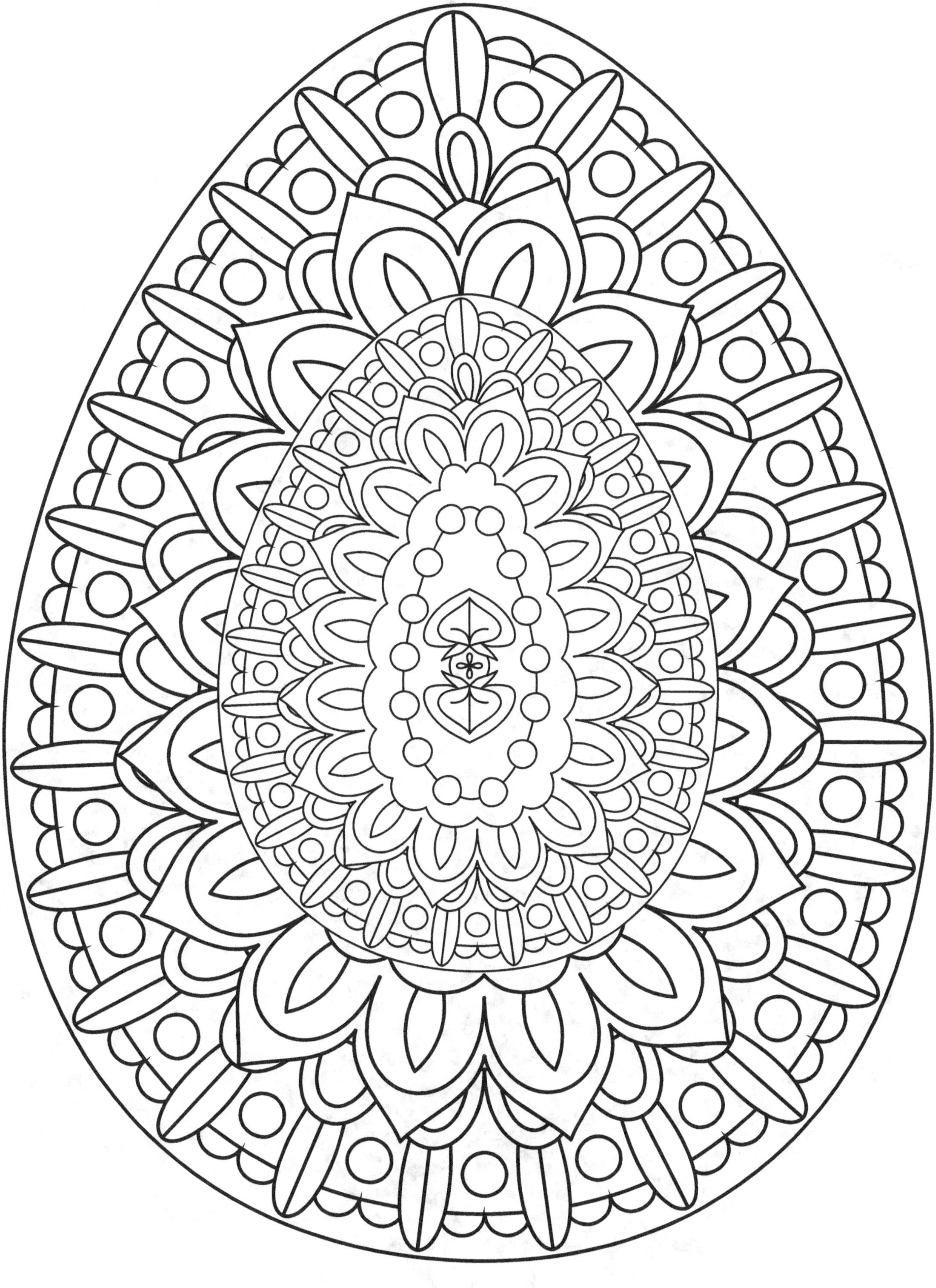

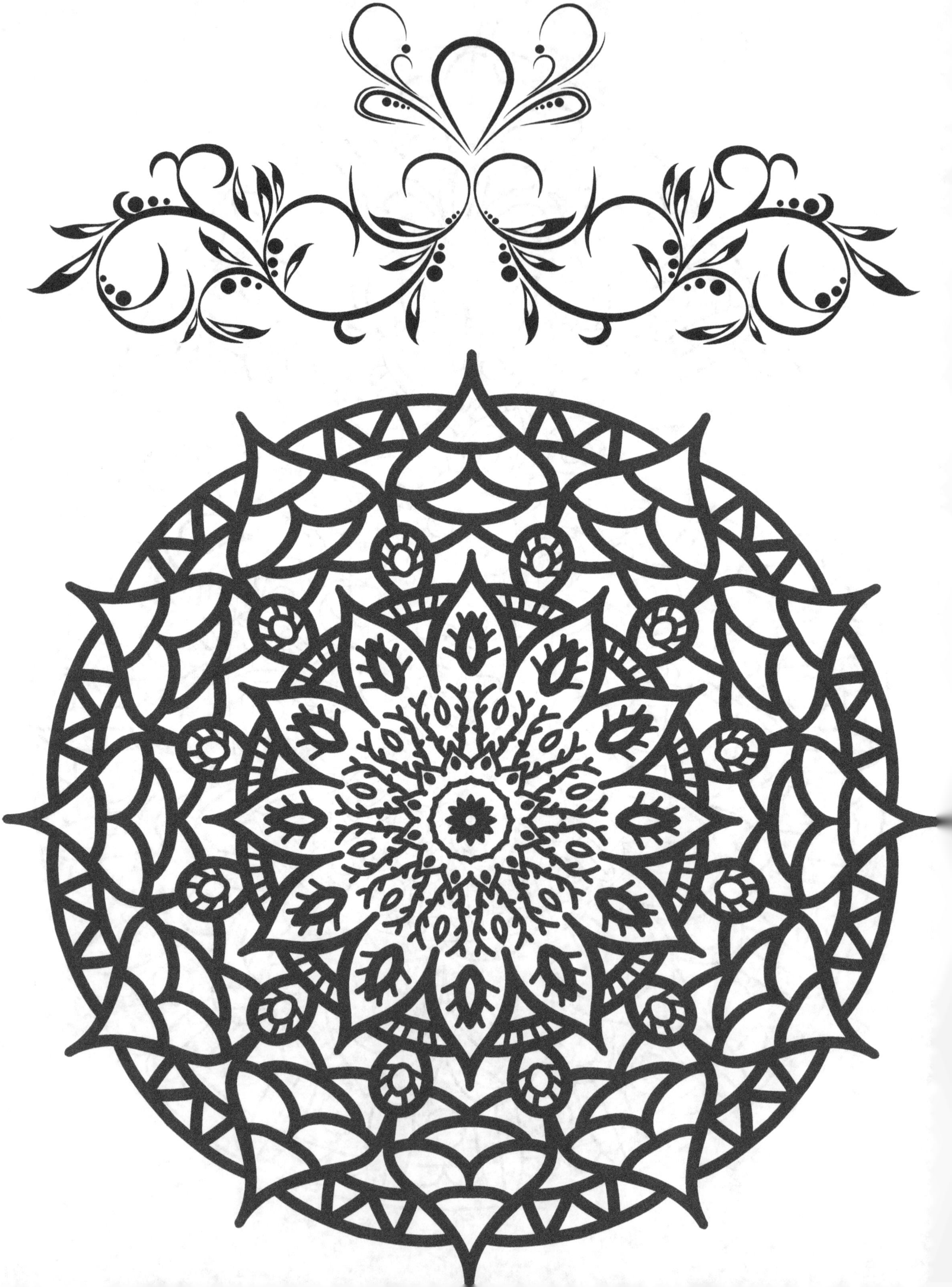

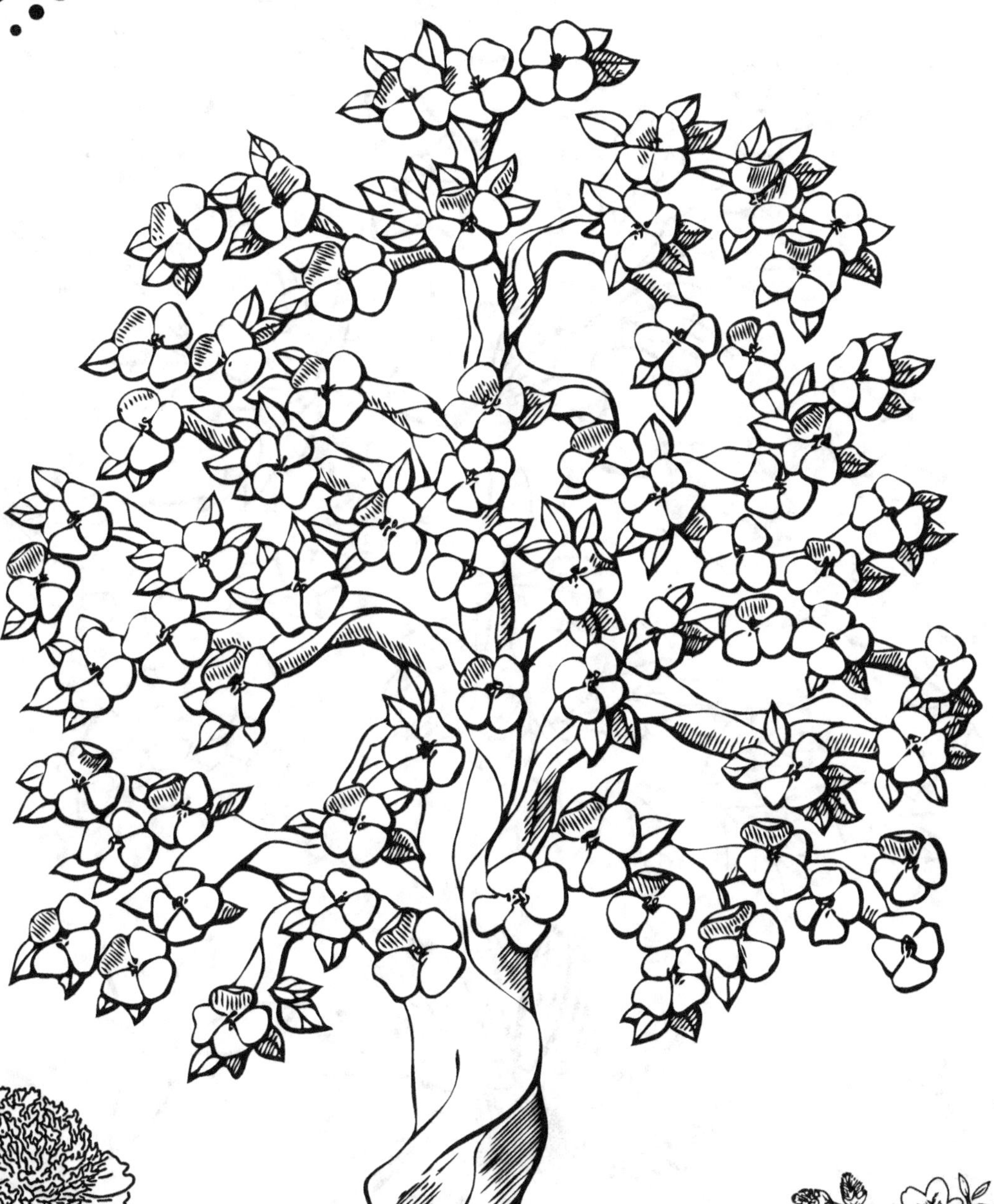
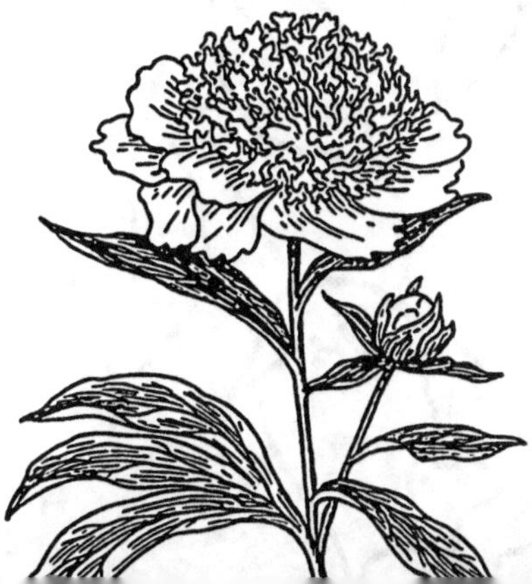
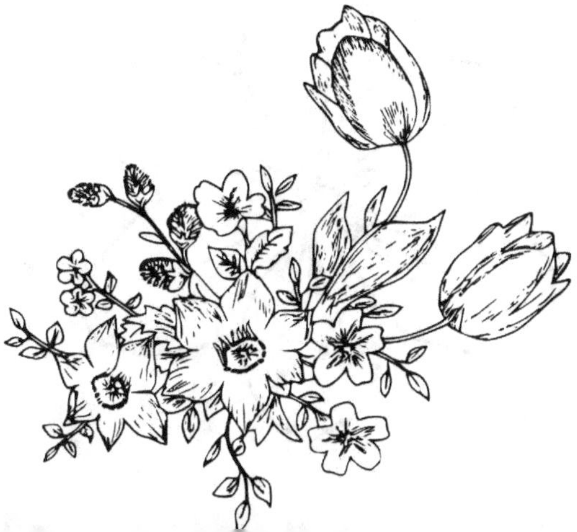

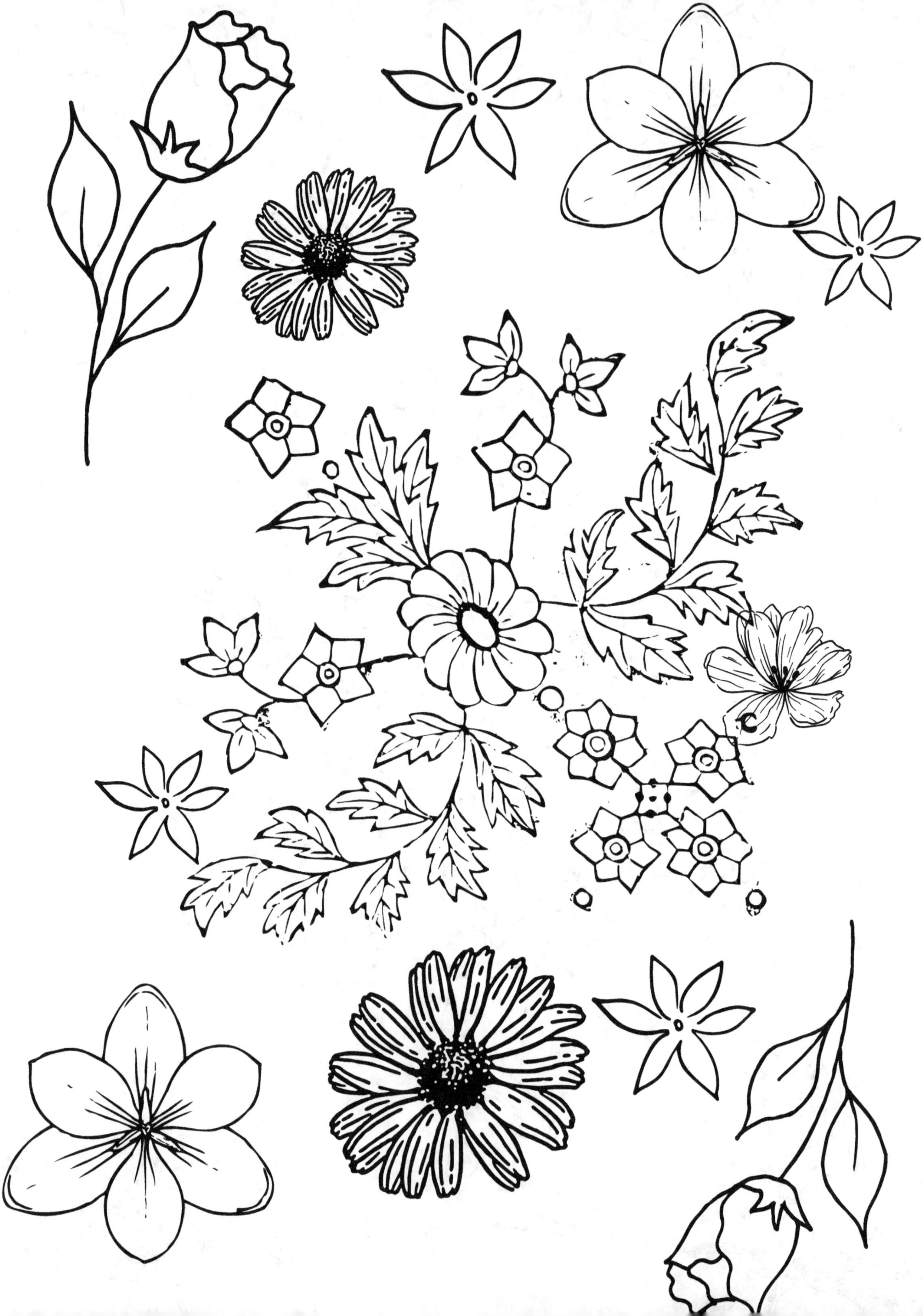

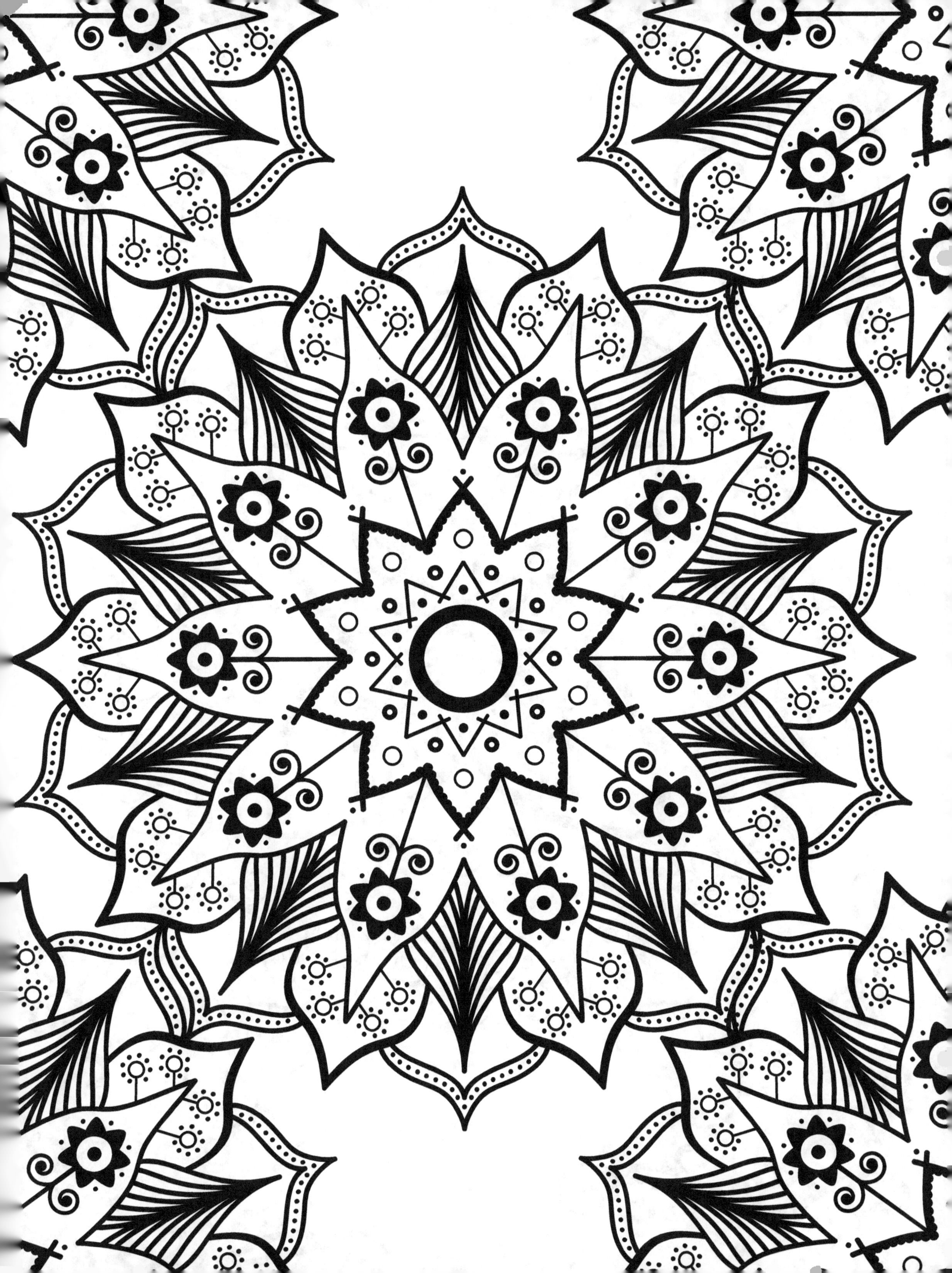

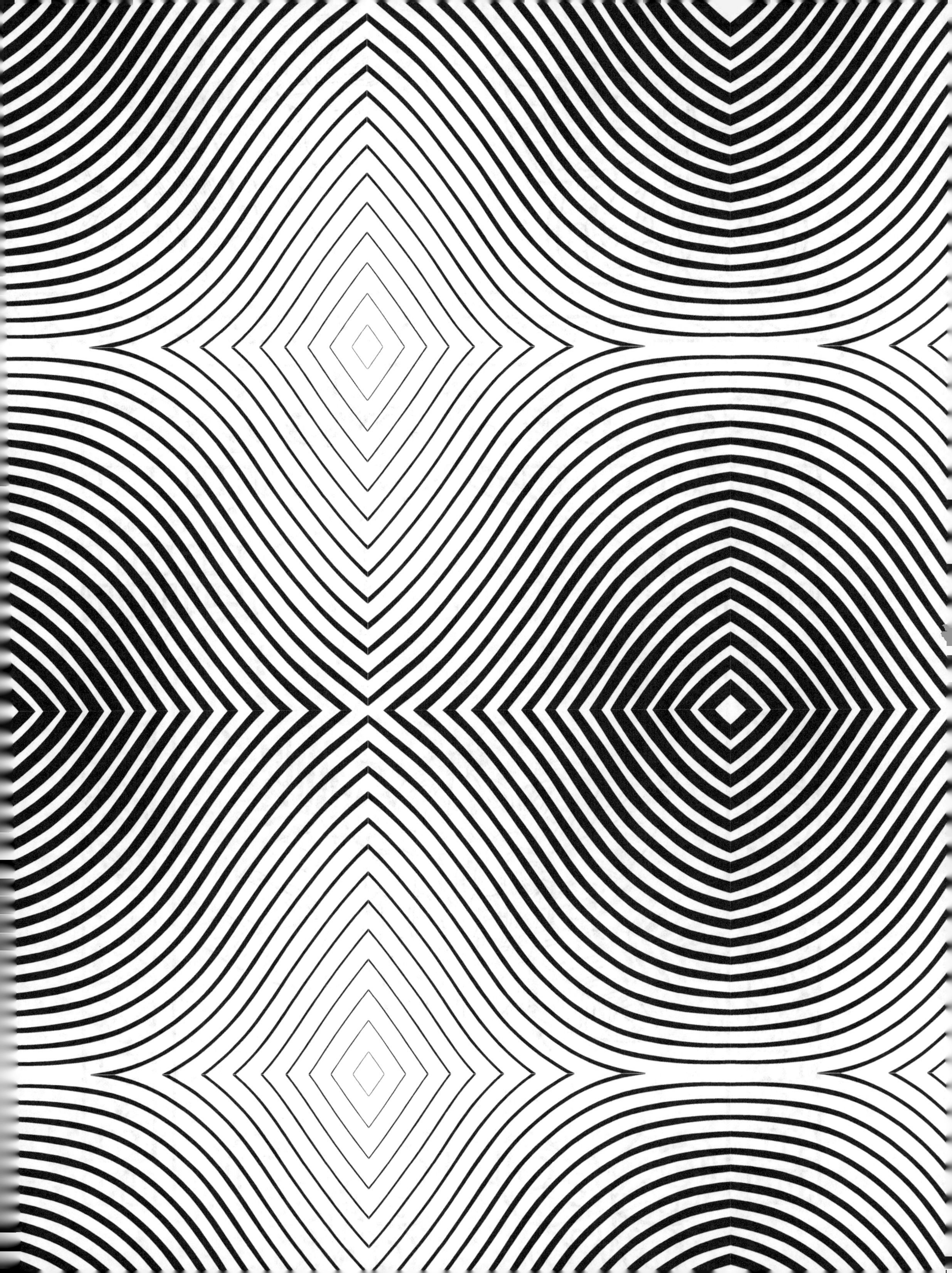

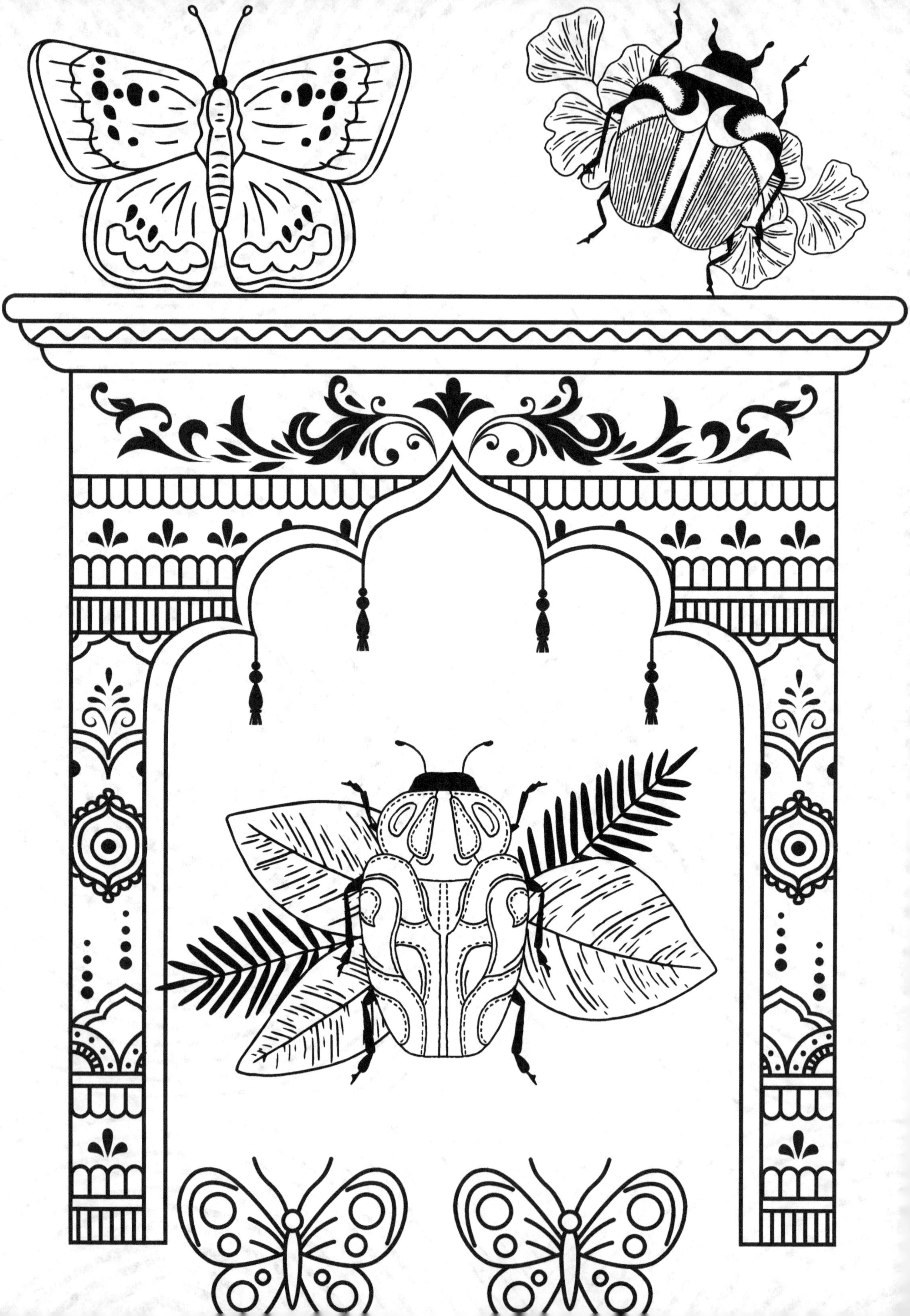

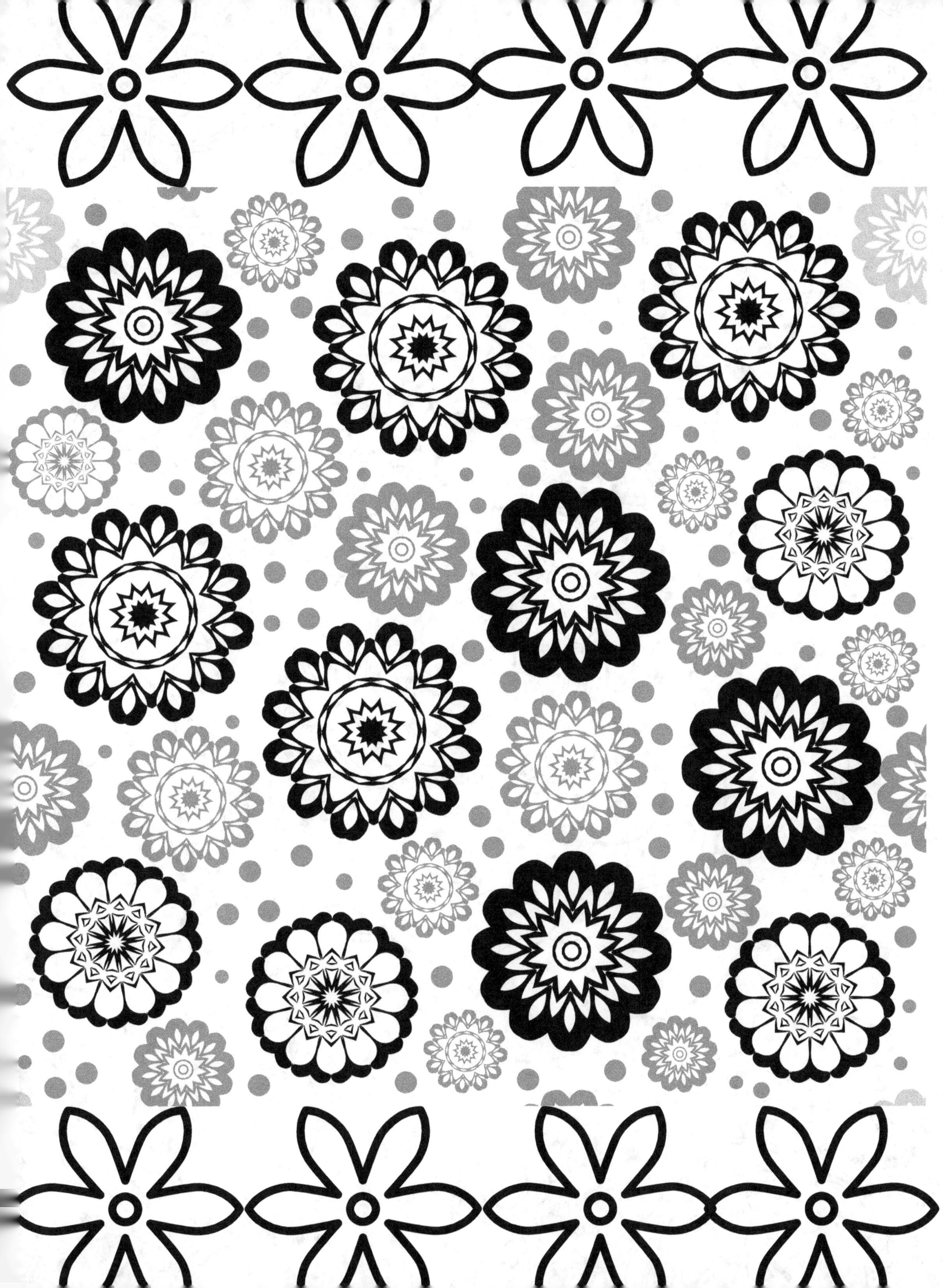

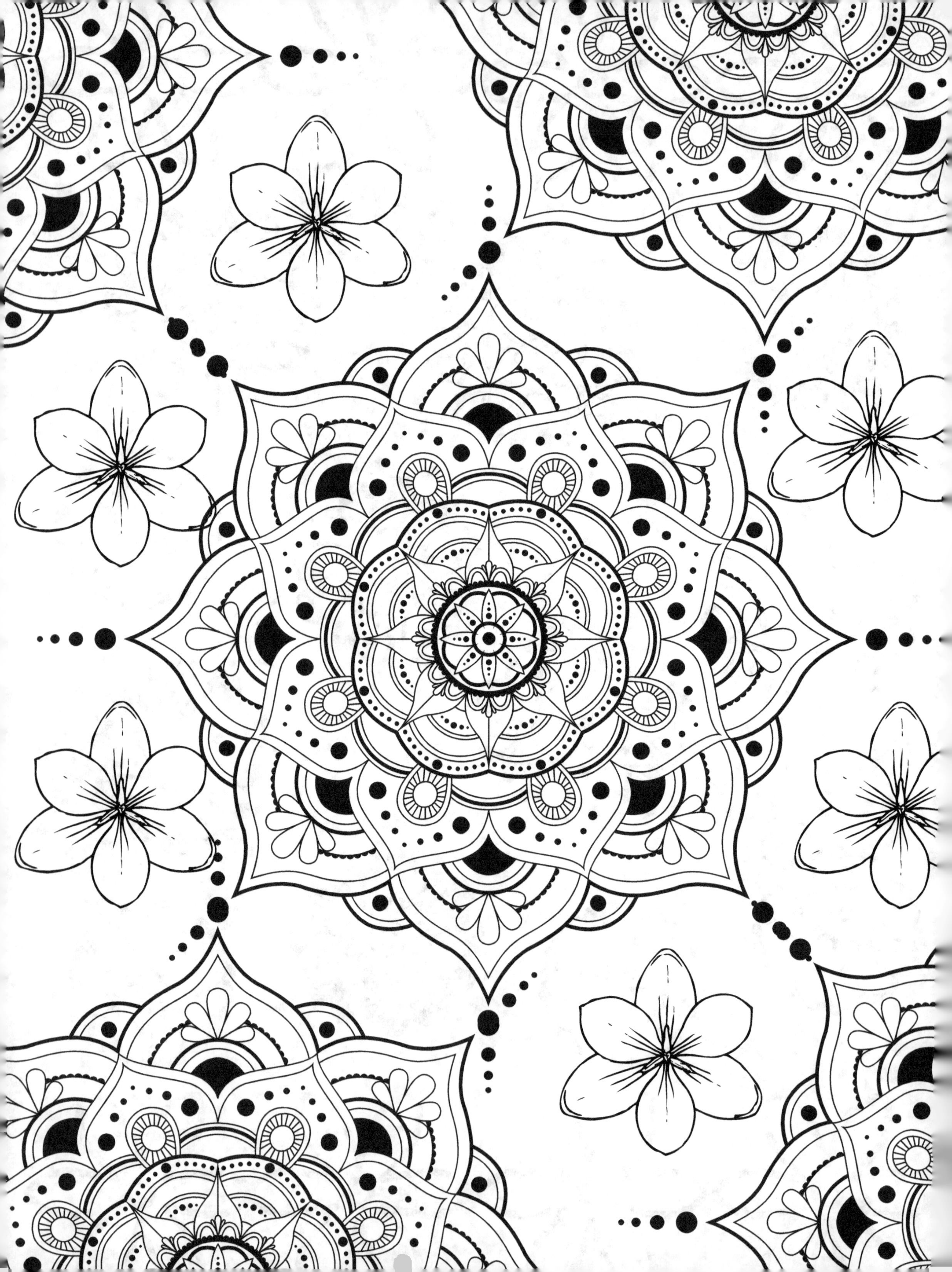

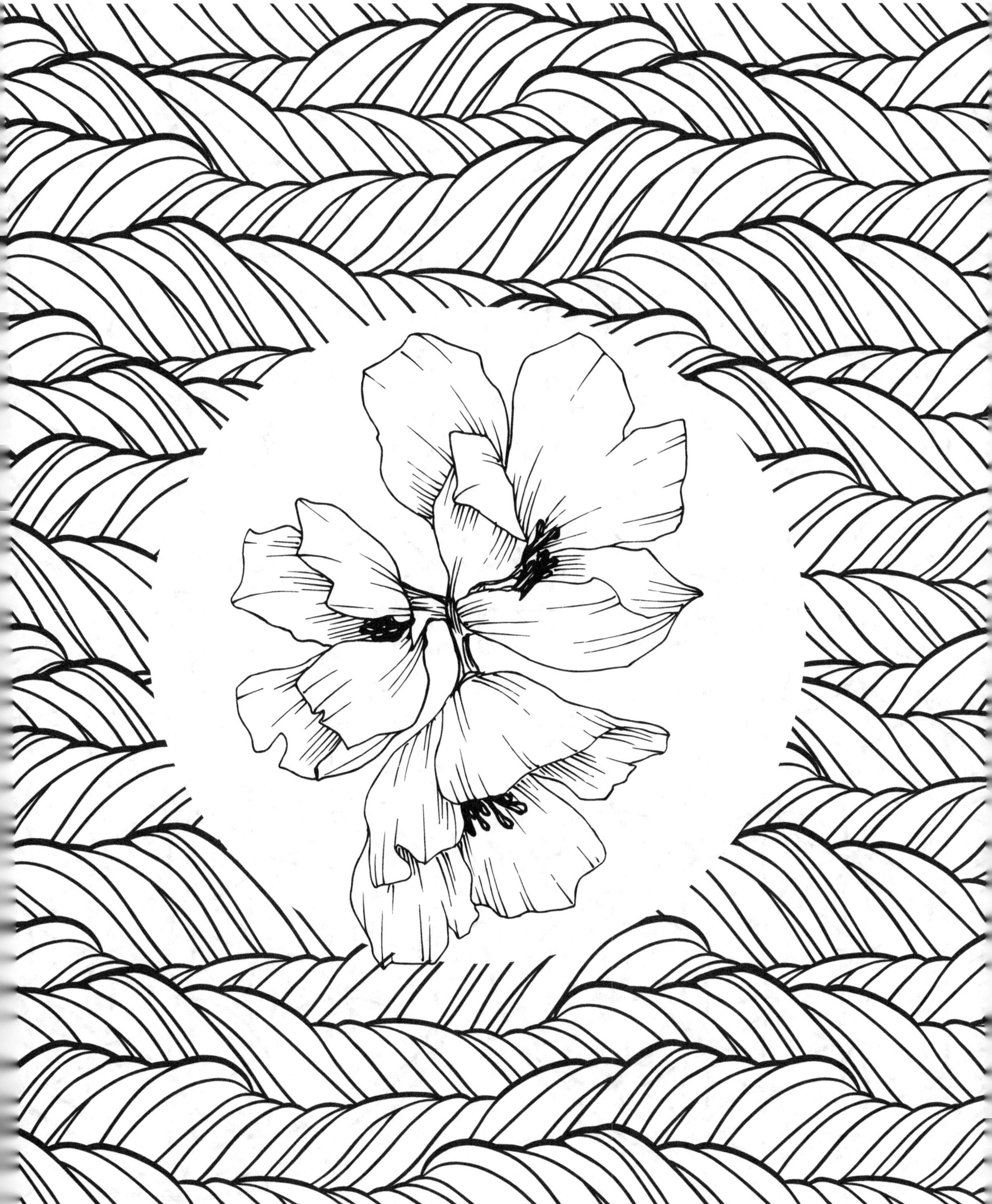

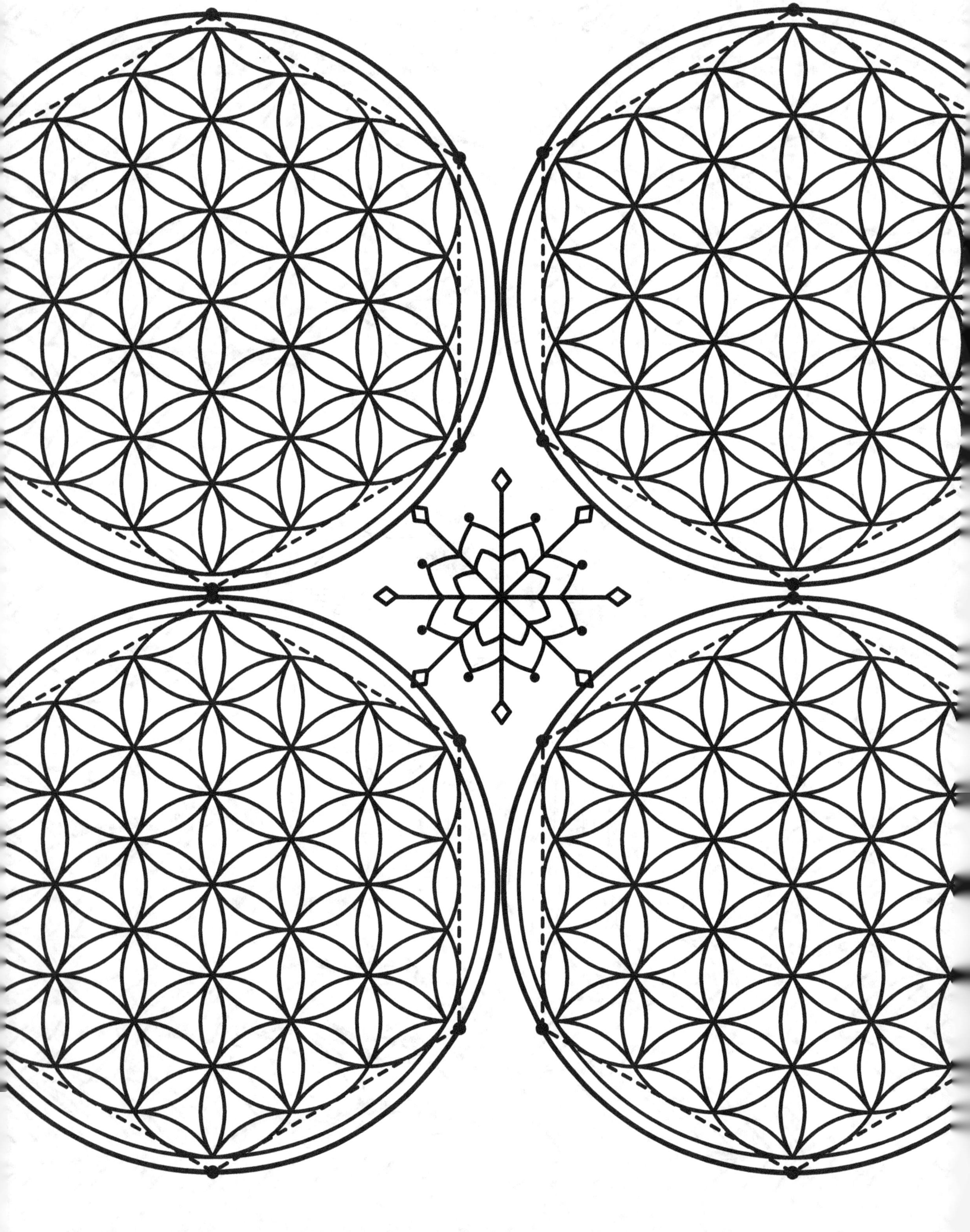

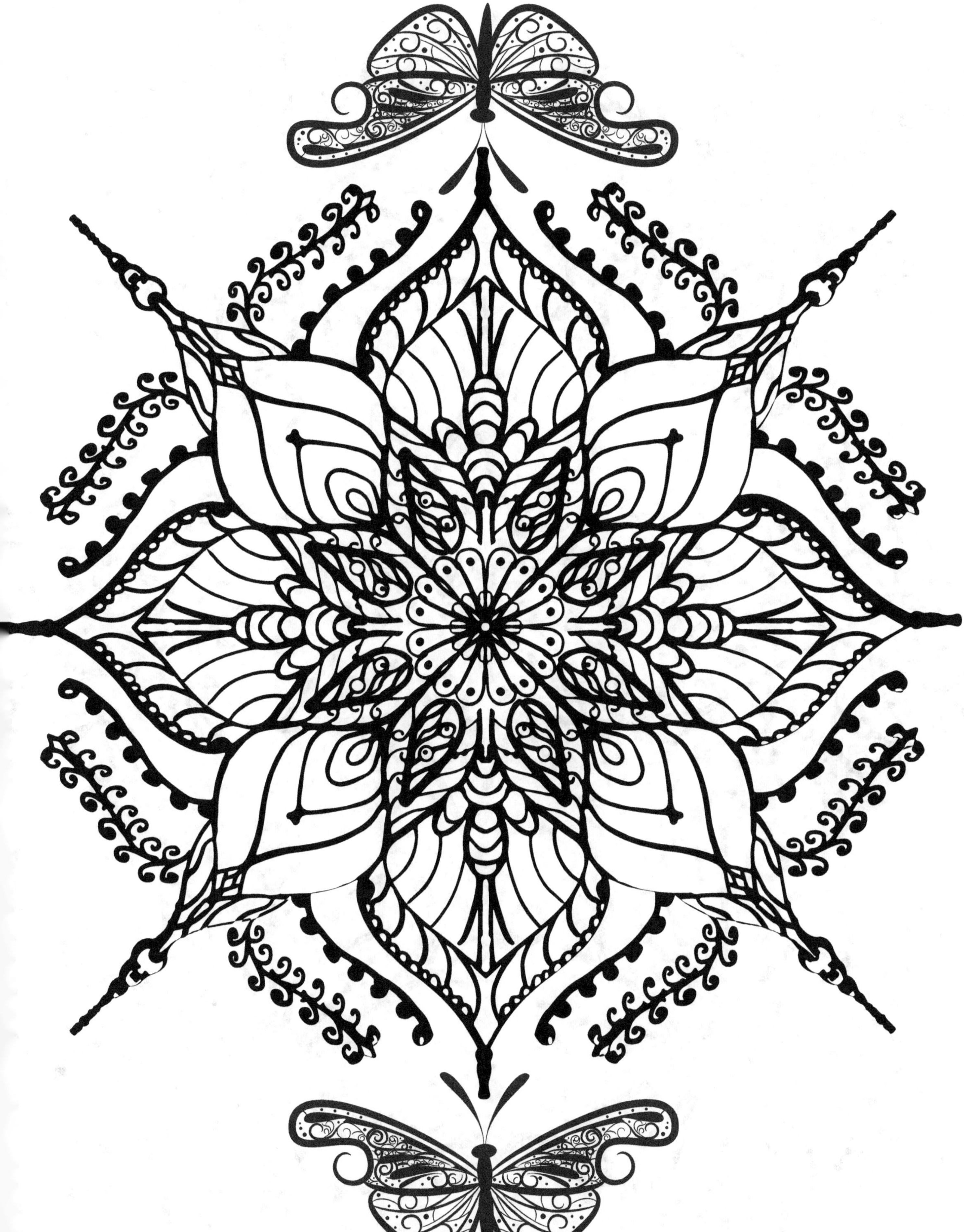

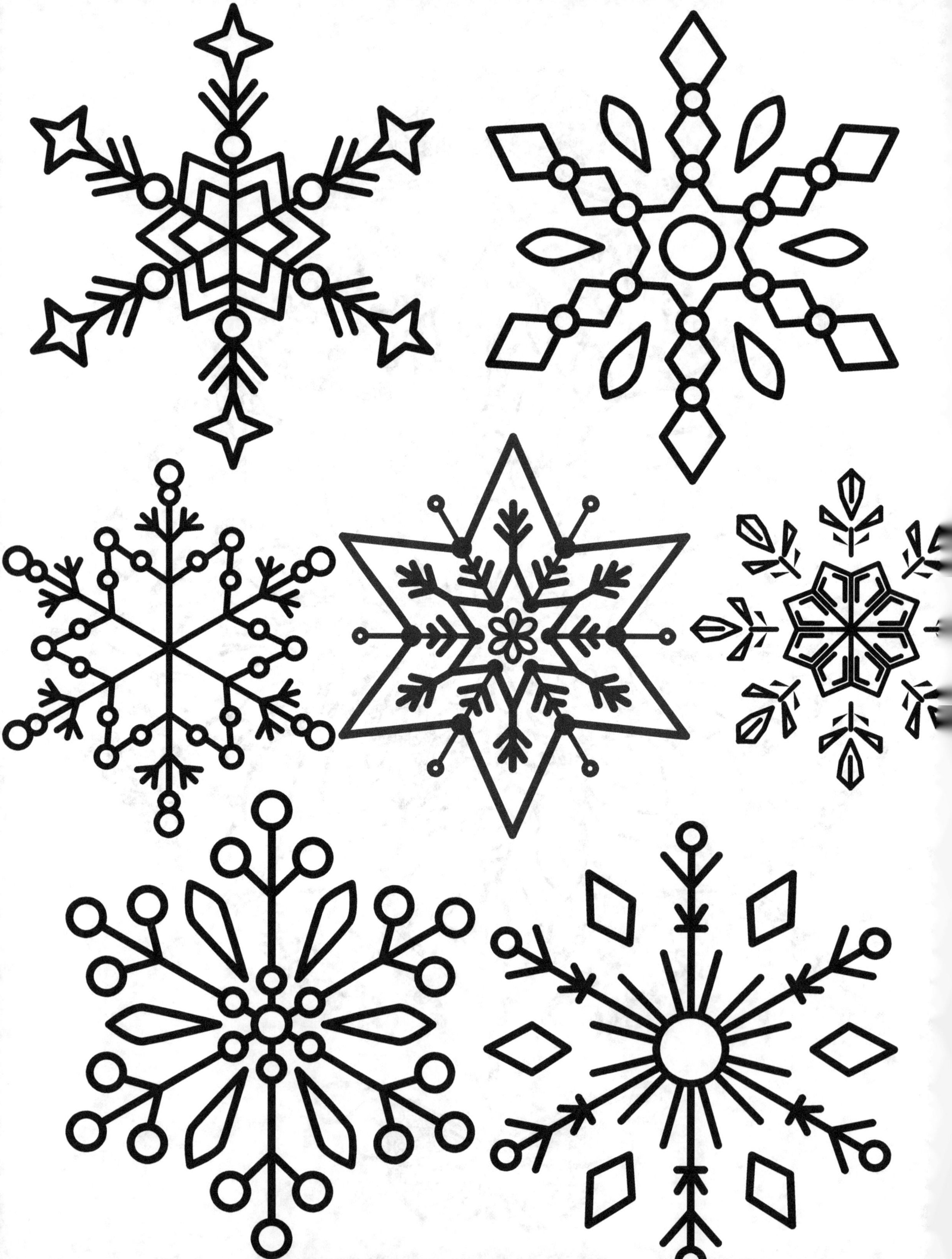

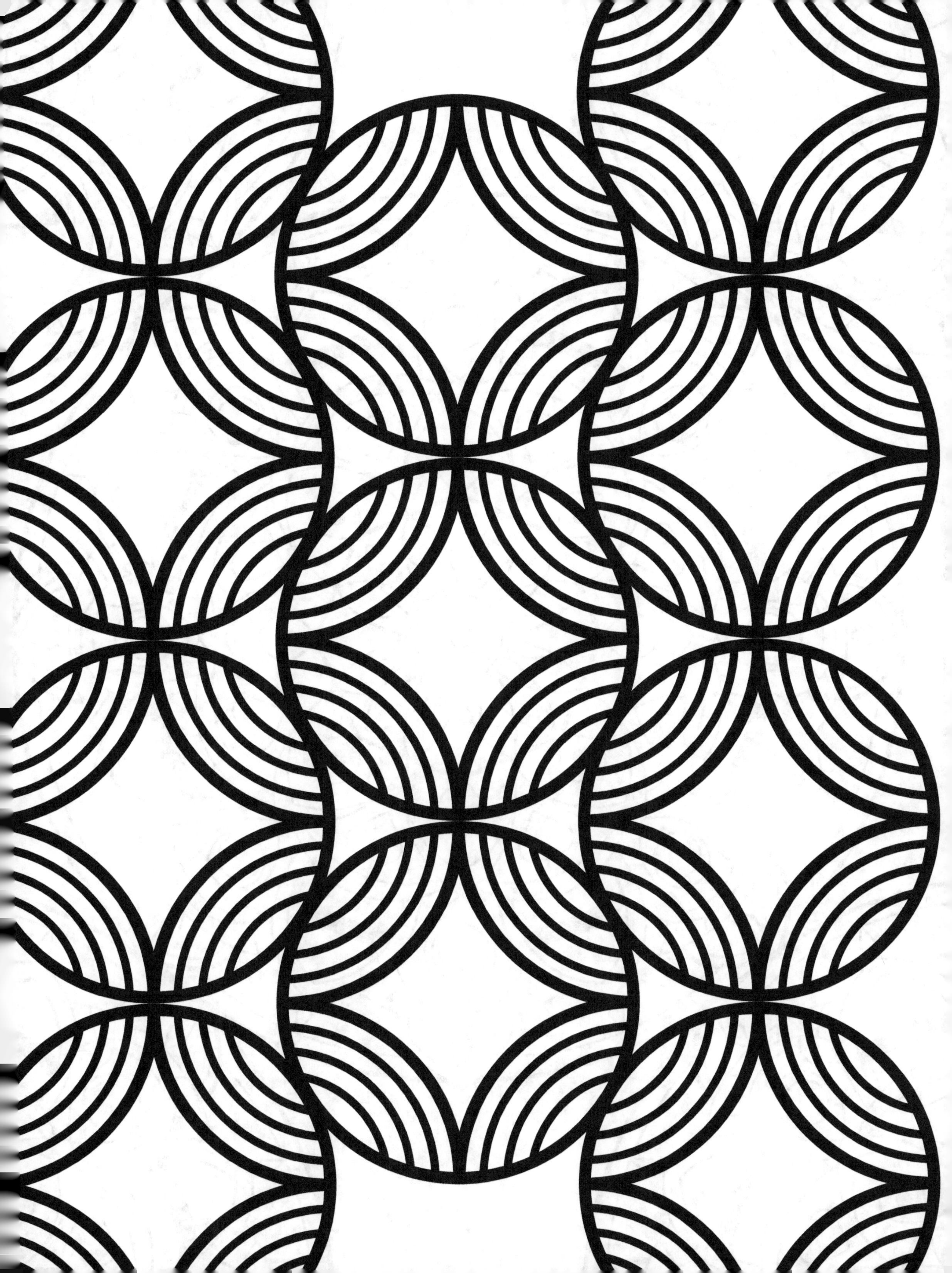

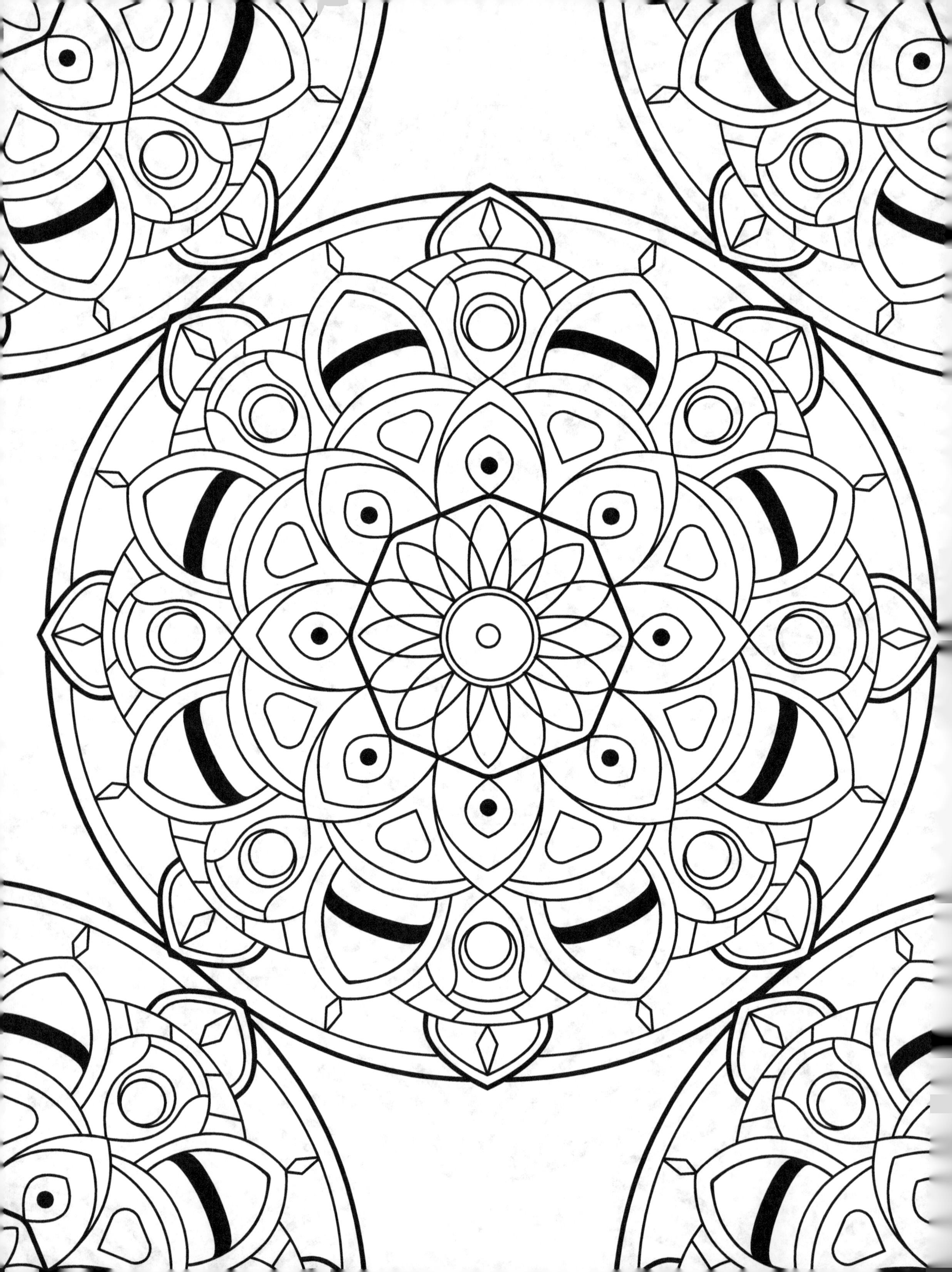

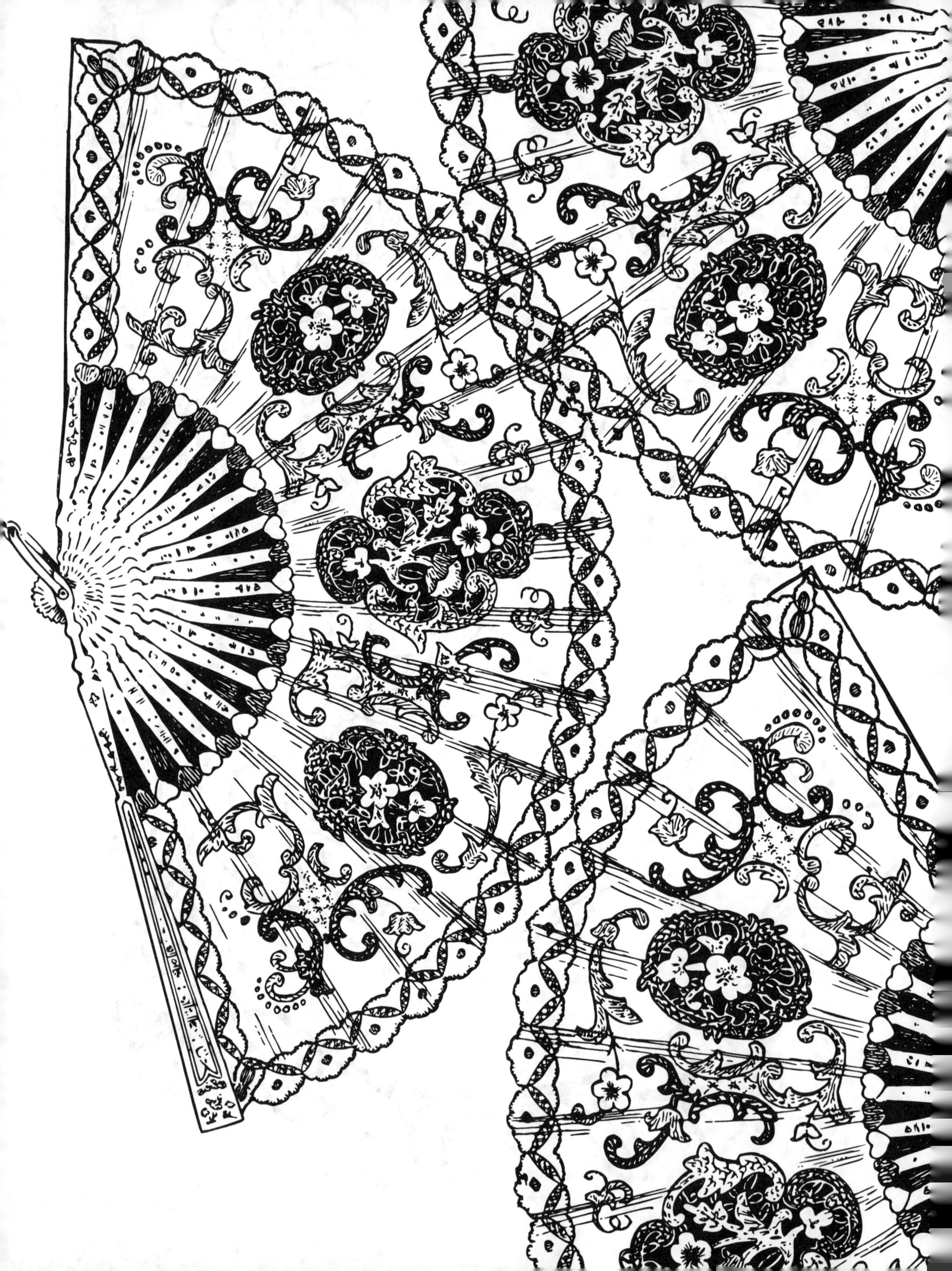

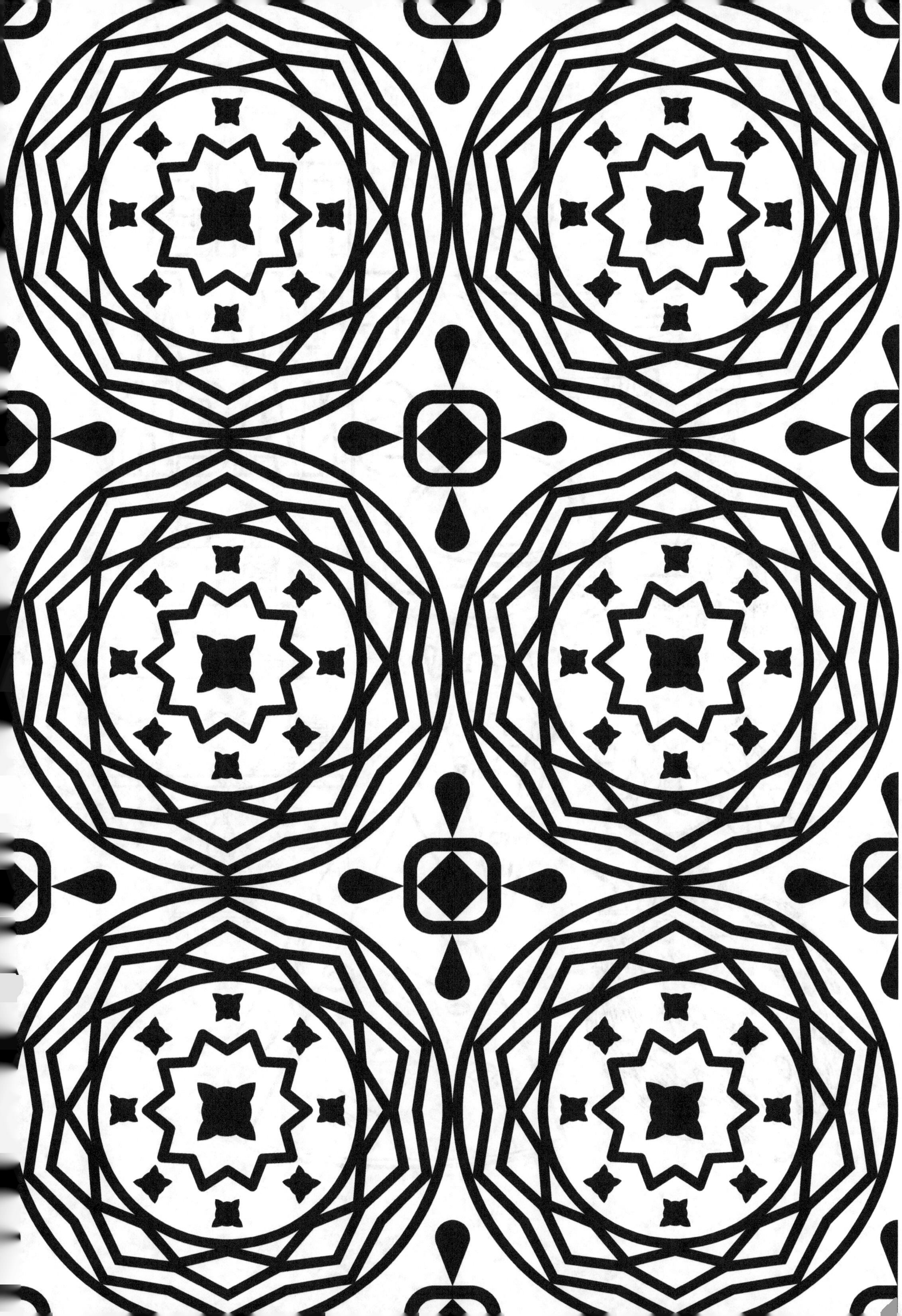

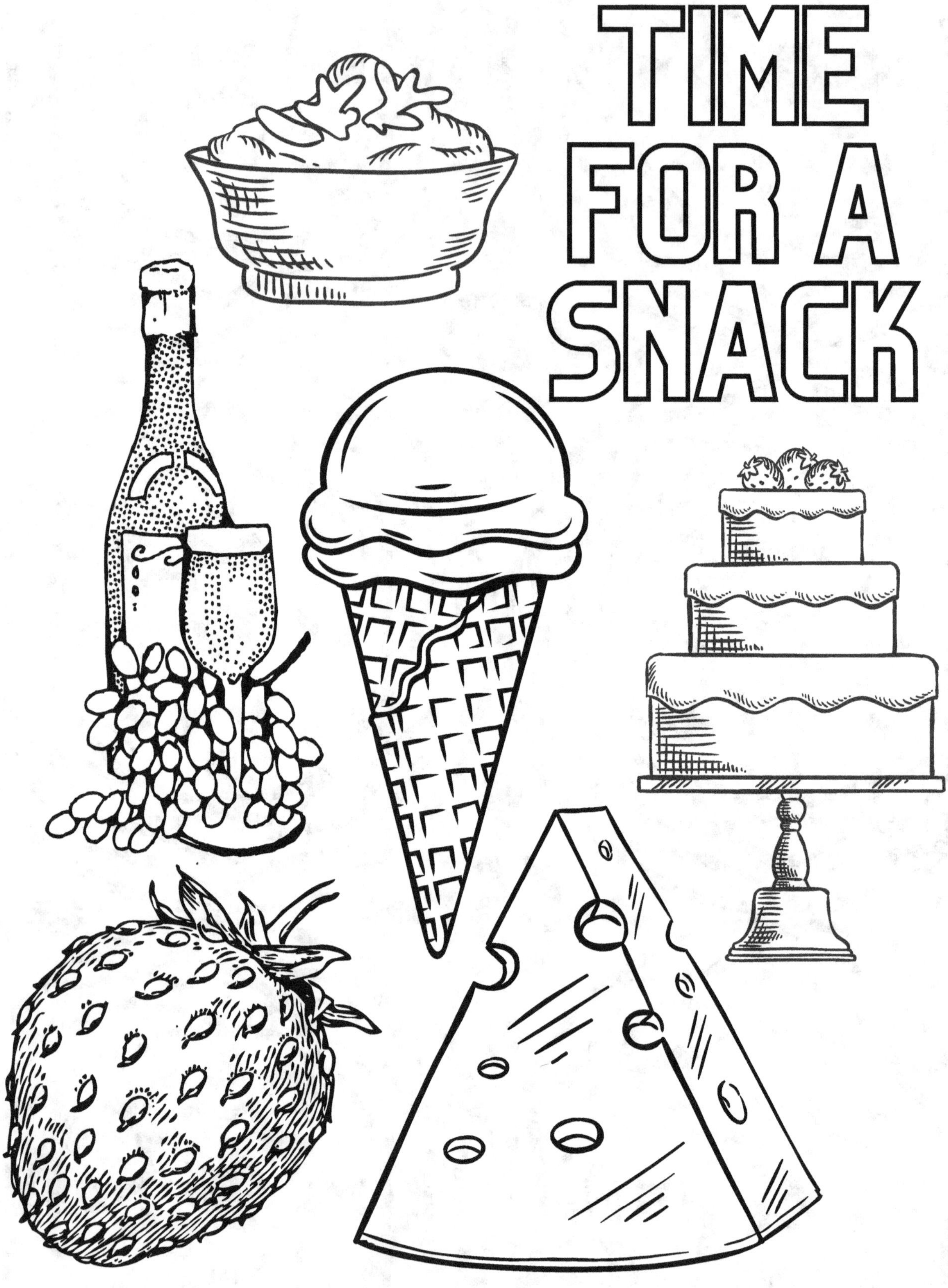
TIME FOR A SNACK

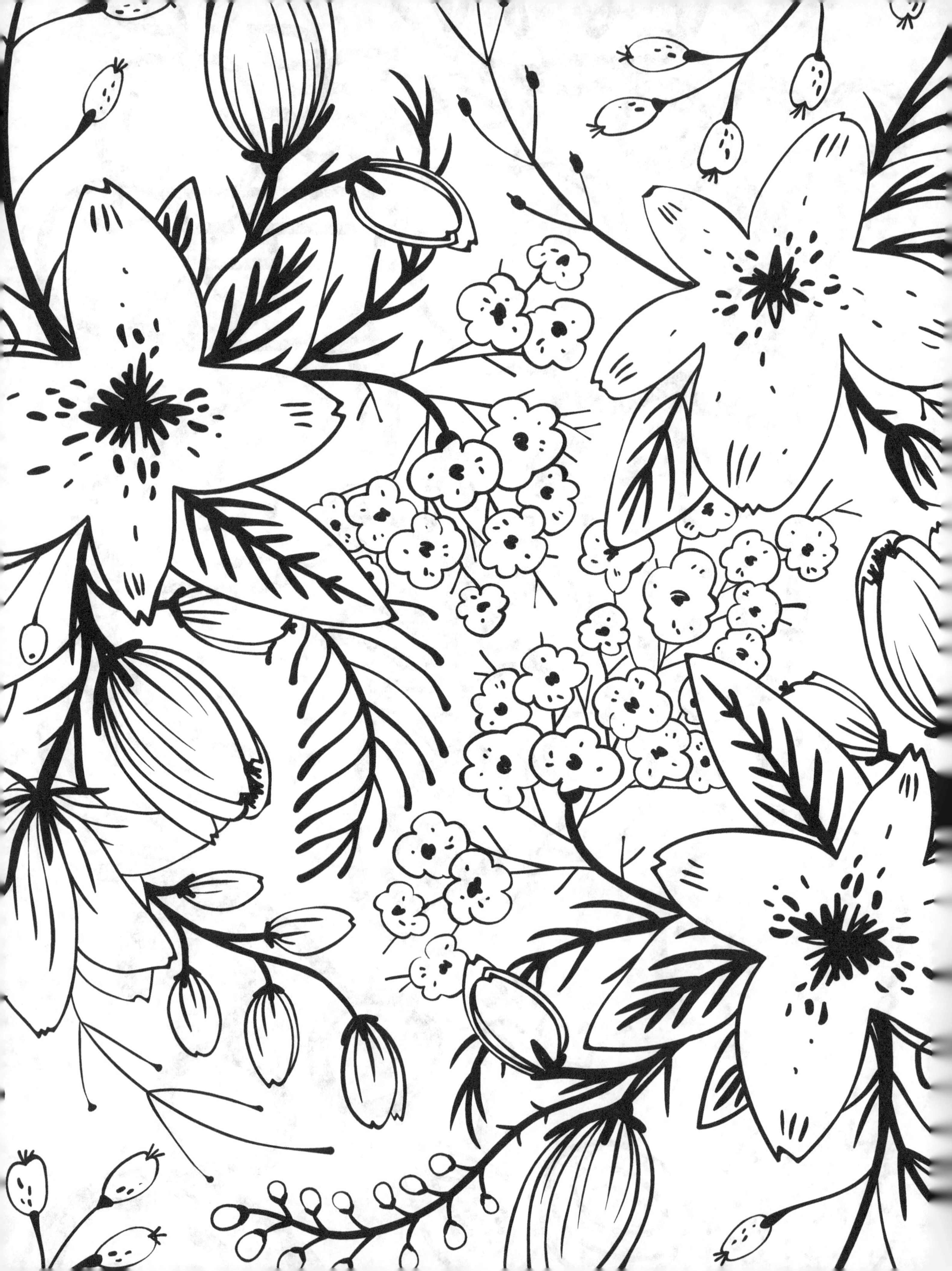

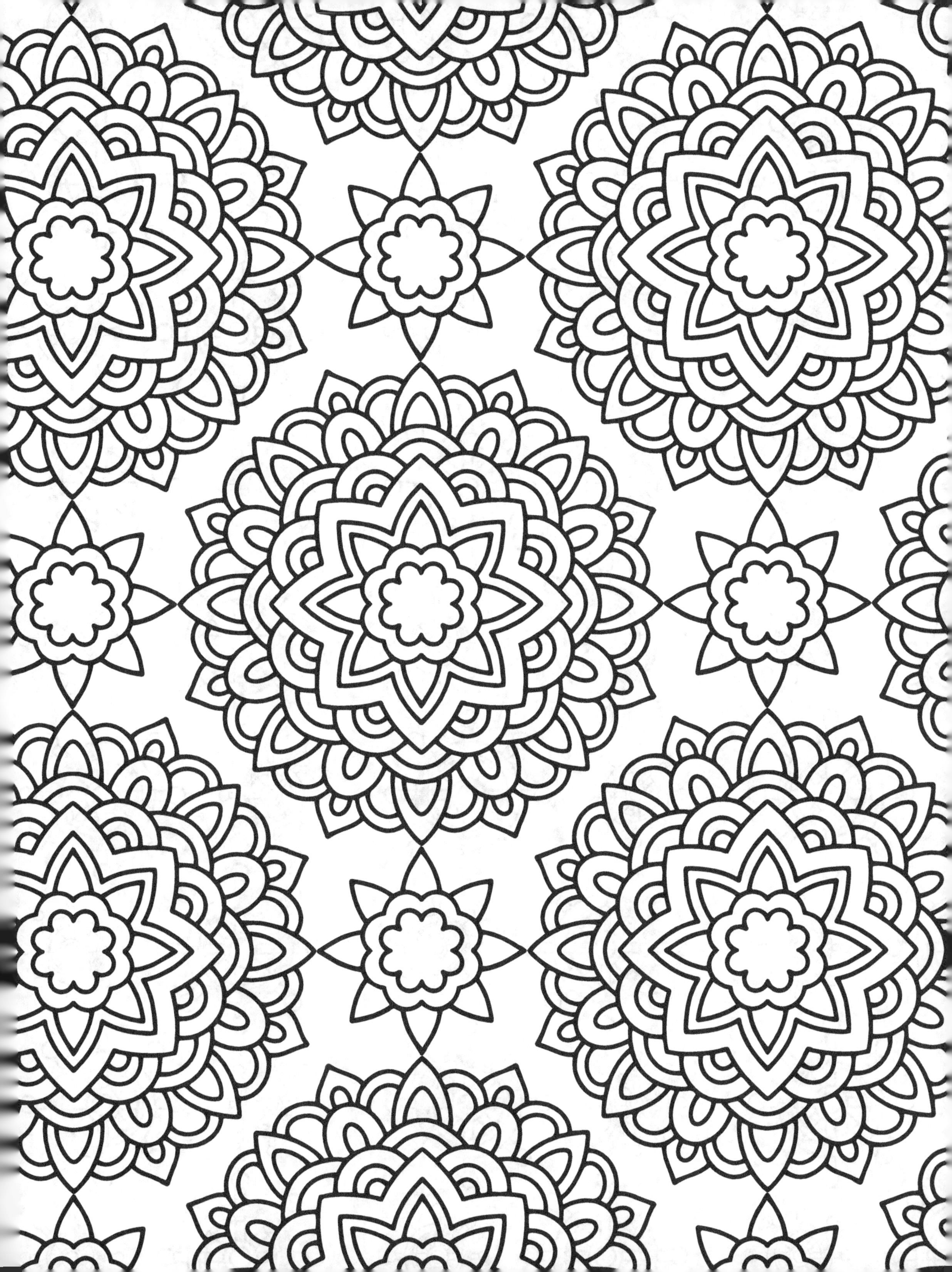

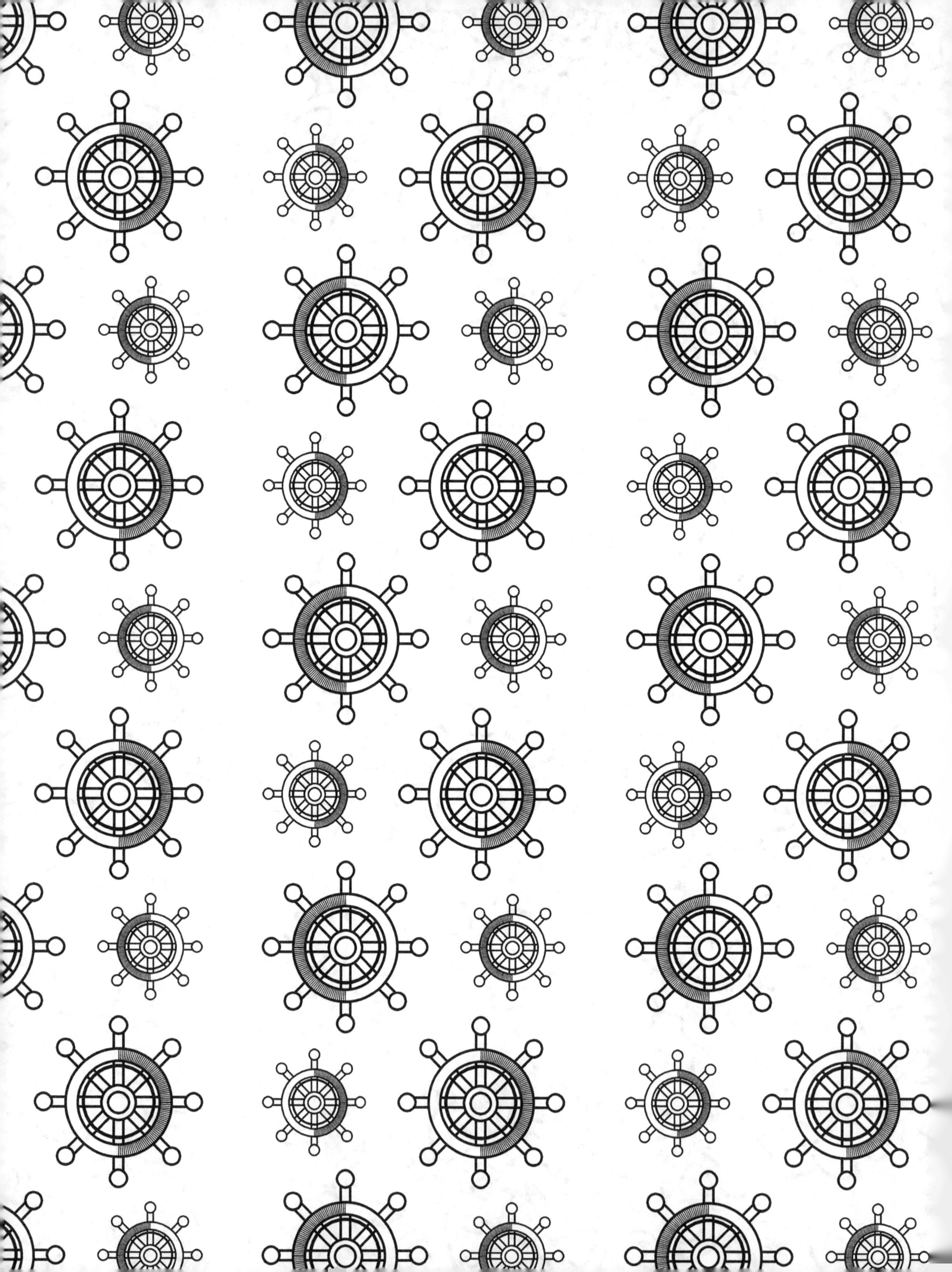

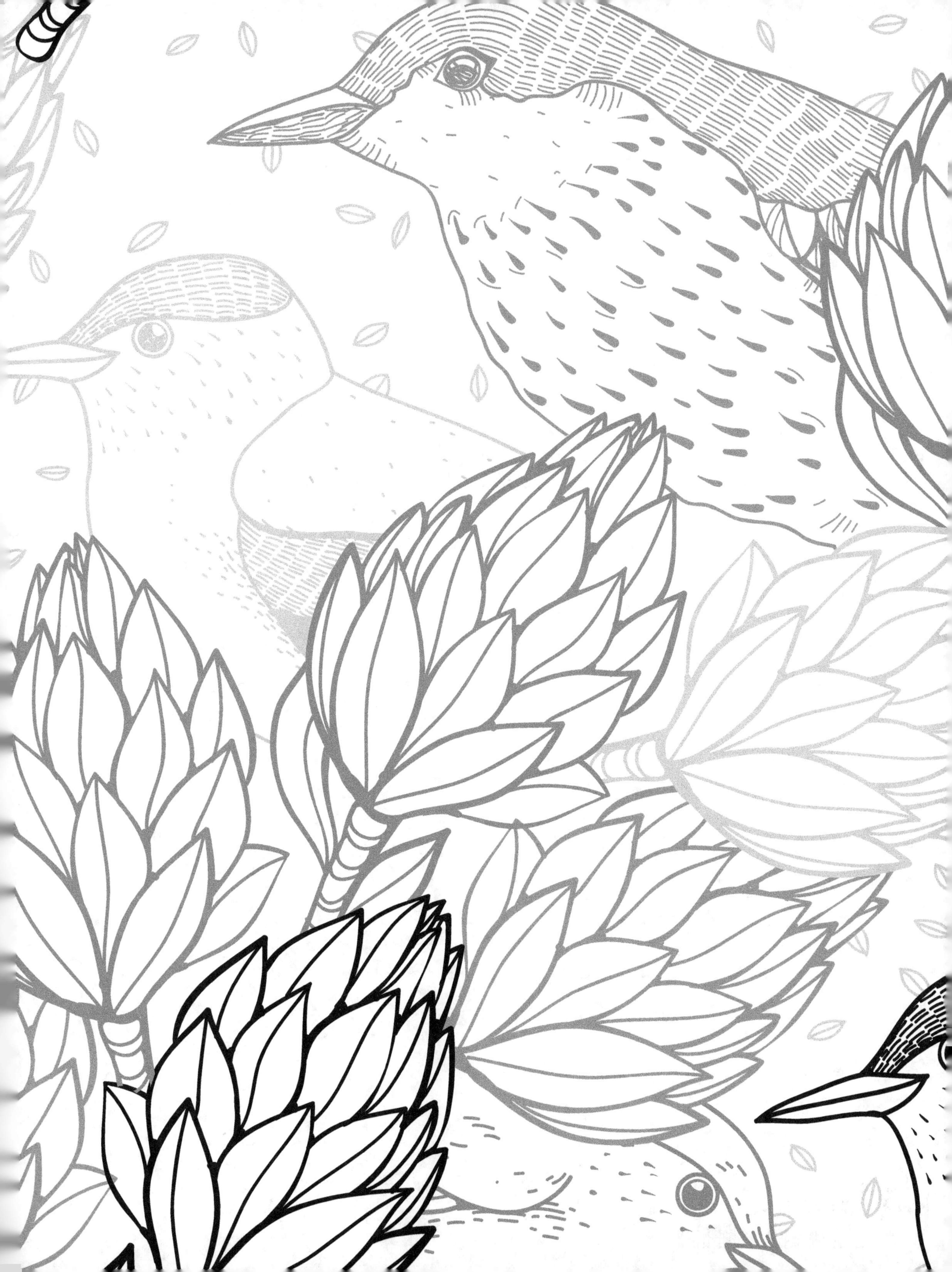

www.ingramcontent.com/pod-product-compliance
Lightning Source LLC
Chambersburg PA
CBHW060436220526
45465CB00008B/3166